Catarina Belo

Ethics and Virtue

Catarina Belo

Ethics and Virtue

Bibliografische Information der Deutschen Nationalbibliothek
Die Deutsche Nationalbibliothek verzeichnet diese Publikation in der Deutschen Nationalbibliografie; detaillierte bibliografische Daten sind im Internet über http://dnb.d-nb.de abrufbar.

Bibliographic information published by the Deutsche Nationalbibliothek
Die Deutsche Nationalbibliothek lists this publication in the Deutsche Nationalbibliografie; detailed bibliographic data are available in the Internet at http://dnb.d-nb.de.

Cover picture: Mata do Fontelo, Viseu, 2020. © copyright 2023 by Duarte Belo. Photo of the author by Ahmad El-Nemr

ISBN: 978-3-95538-041-0

©

Stuttgart 2023

Alle Rechte vorbehalten

Das Werk einschließlich aller seiner Teile ist urheberrechtlich geschützt. Jede Verwertung außerhalb der engen Grenzen des Urheberrechtsgesetzes ist ohne Zustimmung des Verlages unzulässig und strafbar. Dies gilt insbesondere für Vervielfältigungen, Übersetzungen, Mikroverfilmungen und elektronische Speicherformen sowie die Einspeicherung und Verarbeitung in elektronischen Systemen.

All rights reserved. No part of this publication may be reproduced, stored in or introduced into a retrieval system, or transmitted, in any form, or by any means (electronical, mechanical, photocopying, recording or otherwise) without the prior written permission of the publisher. Any person who does any unauthorized act in relation to this publication may be liable to criminal prosecution and civil claims for damages.

Be perfect, as your heavenly Father is perfect.
Matthew 5:48

Table of Contents

Acknowledgments	9
Introduction	11
1. The Nature of Ethics	19
2. The Presuppositions of Ethics	33
2.1. Voluntariness	33
2.2. The Conception of the Good and Happiness	50
2.3. The Challenge of Determinism	88
3. Human Nature	103
3.1. Pleasure, Community and the Emotions	103
3.2. Habit	149
4. The Definition of Virtue	159
4.1. The Unity of the Virtues	196
5. Types of Virtues	199
5.1. Moral and Theological Virtues	199
5.2. The Cardinal Virtues	264
5.3. Friendship	280
5.4. The Intellectual Virtues	315
5.5. Vice	335
Conclusion	343

Acknowledgments

This book was written during a sabbatical leave granted to me by the American University in Cairo in Egypt. During that period, I was based at the Center for Philosophy of the University of Lisbon, in Portugal.

I am grateful to my friend and colleague, Abraham Anderson, for introducing me to Anthony Ashley Cooper, the 3rd Earl of Shaftesbury, when we were both colleagues in teaching at The American University in Cairo from 2006, and for his comments on a previous draft of this book. I am grateful to my friend and colleague, Robin Weiss, for her advice on scholarly literature on Stoicism. I am grateful to my friend and colleague, Marta Mendonça, for her advice on various aspects of modern philosophy.

My friend and colleague, William Melaney, provided detailed comments on a previous draft of this book that were most helpful and for which I am especially grateful.

I am also grateful to Johanna Baboukis for the careful proofreading of the manuscript.

This book is dedicated to my brothers, Diogo and Duarte.

Introduction

Virtue ethics is a branch of ethics which in recent times has returned to the center of the attention of philosophers, in particular ethicists. Virtue ethics was the dominant approach to ethics in the Western tradition since Greek antiquity and through to the modern period. The theme of virtue, including particular virtues, is the subject of several Platonic dialogues, and is an enduring theme in Socrates' and Plato's philosophy as a whole. For Aristotle too, ethics and ethical action are centered around the theme of virtue, and the particular virtues. Virtue plays a central role in the various schools of Hellenistic philosophy. This tradition continues into the Patristic and the Scholastic periods of the history of philosophy and the Renaissance. Within classical or medieval Islamic philosophy, virtue is also the focus of research on ethics, in particular the works of Alfarabi, Averroes and Miskawayh, among others, and virtue is also central to the ethical thought of Maimonides. In so far as virtue ethics, with its focus on virtue, represents an emphasis on the personal moral qualities of individuals, other kinds of ethics, Hindu, Buddhist or Confucian, can also be considered as forming part of virtue ethics.

Within the Western tradition, virtue ethics remained alive and thrived into the modern period, in particular among the British moralists, such as Shaftesbury and Hume. Kant's orientation of ethics towards the principle of duty and the establishment of universal principles of conduct, rather than highlighting particular qualities of the human subject, effectively altered the dominance of virtue ethics, turning the attention of ethical studies to deontology and the notion of duty. Some contemporary scholars oppose the two kinds of ethics, one which highlights personal qualities of the ethical subject, and the other which insists on universal duties which are independent of particular circumstances or particular individuals. In contemporary scholarship, one finds studies arguing for the compatibility between virtue ethics and the universal notion of duty and norms.

The current revival of virtue ethics has been attributed to analytic philosophy, and in particular Anscombe and her influential paper 'Modern Moral Philosophy', which delineates the differences between duty ethics and virtue ethics. Other studies followed, such as MacIntyre's *After Virtue*. There are currently many studies, including book-length studies on virtue ethics, and also on particular virtues and the significance of virtue within contemporary discourses on ethics. These studies build on the previous tradition of virtue ethics and seek to highlight its significance for contemporary ethical life.

Virtue is a topic which concerns human behavior as a whole and thus concerns central aspects of human life. A topic related to virtue and ethics more generally is politics and the law. The inextricable link between virtue and politics is already present in Plato's and Aristotle's works, both of whom stress the need for virtuous behavior by individuals in their personal relations and within the political state. For Aristotle, the study of ethics is preliminary to the study of politics.

Another issue that is almost always associated with virtue is happiness. Already for the ancient Greek and Hellenistic philosophers, virtue was a means to happiness or identical to happiness itself. These two related issues will be treated in this work, although only in so far as they pertain to the broader theme of virtue.

The present work, composed as a philosophical dialogue, builds on a previous philosophical dialogue of mine, titled *Spirit in Philosophy: A Metaphysical Inquiry* (Stuttgart, WiSa, 2019), which includes a subchapter on ethics. In the present work, I follow the same format, namely that of the philosophical dialogue, which affords a certain kind of freedom and flexibility in tackling various philosophical topics. In addition, I build on the conclusions reached in that work, regarding the significance of a spiritual or idealist approach to ethics, the concept of the good and the final cause as central to ethics, the need to understand human nature in developing an ethical theory, and more broadly the notion of causality and agency as pivotal to debates on ethics.

Contemporary scholars often distinguish between virtue theory and virtue ethics, the former consisting in a clarification of what virtue means and its place within ethical theories, and the latter making the case for virtue as the most suitable approach for producing good ethical conduct. In this sense, virtue ethics is opposed to other ethics theories such as duty ethics and consequentialism or utilitarianism, which measure the goodness of an action based on its results, to the exclusion, for instance, of the means involved in bringing about an action. This work will make a case for virtue ethics as the most natural and productive form of ethics.

Virtue ethics is characterized by a focus on individual behavior and its improvement, although its consequences are far from being individualistic or particular. Virtuous practice can be found at the communal level or in society as a whole, but virtue is considered to develop first at the level of the individual. In the *Republic*, Plato famously makes parallelisms between virtue, in particular justice, in the soul, as the harmony between the various faculties, and virtue in the state as the harmony between the different classes of citizens. This parallelism is taken up by Alfarabi in his *Aphorisms of the Statesman* and *The Principles of the Opinions of the Inhabitants of the Virtuous City* which describes the significance of virtue for the individual and for the state. Without diminishing the significance of virtuous action for the political state, Aristotle holds that virtuous behavior pertains to individuals and has to take account of their circumstances. Nevertheless, he also thinks of ethics as being the first part of politics, and views the link between the two disciplines as continuous.

While tackling related issues such as happiness, considered to be the goal of virtue, and the role of virtue in society and in politics, this work will above all study virtue as an individual endeavor and goal, and more specifically virtue theory as a set of general principles which help each individual to act in a moral way.

As with *Spirit in Philosophy: A Metaphysical Inquiry*, this work draws heavily on the history of philosophy. While it would be difficult to convey all the conceptions of virtue to be found within the history of philosophy, it is important to take account of the most salient ones, on the one hand, in order to avoid unwittingly repeating what has already been said, and on the other, to build on that rich tradition. This study draws inspiration particularly from the works of Aristotle, Saint Thomas Aquinas and Shaftesbury. Among contemporary philosophers the works of Terence Irwin and Linda Zagzebski are particularly helpful.

Aristotle builds on Plato's discussion of virtue in his dialogues. These dialogues, especially those which are considered to be the early Platonic dialogues, analyze specific virtues, such as piety, friendship, courage and justice, while seeking their precise definitions. One dialogue, the *Meno*, is centered around virtue itself, and how it can be defined. Some related debates discuss the connection between virtue and the soul, virtue and knowledge, and the unity of the virtues. Naturally, Socrates is the protagonist in Plato's dialogues, and some scholars have sought to distinguish his views from those of Plato. However, even the middle dialogues, in which Plato appears to develop his own philosophy and distinct theories, have virtue as the focus of the discussions.

Aristotle, as a historian of philosophy and a former student of Plato, develops his own theory of virtue and his own virtue ethics. Some of the hallmarks of Aristotle's virtue ethics consist in considering virtue as a result of habituation, as a middle term between extremes and as a requisite for happiness. However, like Plato he views virtue as residing in the human soul and as a characteristic of human excellence. Later, the Stoics identify virtue with knowledge and state that virtue suffices for attaining happiness, and their views are analyzed by ancient, medieval and modern philosophers.

Saint Thomas Aquinas, as an Aristotelian philosopher and a Christian theologian, brings together various aspects of Aristotelian virtue ethics and develops them in tandem with a reflection on God's role in laying down the religious and moral law, and as a model for human virtue. In particular, Aquinas develops the notion of voluntary action, the connection between virtue and the law, as well as those virtues which are distinctively theological.

Shaftesbury is an important representative of the emphasis on the role of emotion in ethics, as well as the aesthetic appreciation of virtue, and therefore foreshadows current reflections on the link between human nature and moral action. His reflections on human nature and the role of religion in shaping moral habits are also central to his philosophy. Many other philosophers wrote about virtue, and several of them will be mentioned later in this work.

Naturally, ethics is a very broad field, consisting of several branches. Even virtue ethics can be understood in different ways, as it has been by many different philosophers. It can be explored in connection with human nature in all its complexity, human action and normative questions. Therefore, it is important to introduce some central and broad questions within the field of ethics before entering issues pertaining specifically to virtue ethics, and making a case for virtue ethics in relation to other branches of normative ethics. Virtue ethics includes many issues broadly pertaining to ethics, and philosophers who have developed this theory have tended to describe ideal human behavior and character.

1. The Nature of Ethics

Student: Ethics is an important branch of philosophy, which was and remains a central aspect of philosophical reflection.

Teacher: Ethics is a central branch of philosophy. In certain senses, it can be considered as an independent discipline, that is to say, independent of philosophy, especially when combined with the natural sciences, such as biology. When we think of bioethics, for instance, we think of a separate discipline with its own principles and conclusions, and its own subdisciplines. Bioethics by itself is a very rich field of research, and it is constantly being enriched by new discoveries in biology. However, as a part of ethics, bioethics is one of the several disciplines belonging to ethics. Applied ethics in turn points to the application of ethics to particular problems and disciplines, such as for instance business ethics, which studies business practices and how they can be improved.

Many disciplines became independent of philosophy beginning in the Renaissance, but this was due to a greater role of experimentation in those sciences, which came to set their own principles, and developed their own research and experimentation methods, based on the scientific method. Ethics, in its theoretical and practical aspects, is still a speculative discipline, and so it remains a part of philosophy. Interestingly, metaethics, which examines the foundations of ethical thought and the pertinence and meaning of the questions debated within ethics, such as moral value, and the circumstances within which ethical action is understood, is also part of philosophy.

Student: Are there other reasons why ethics remains a part of philosophy, in comparison with other disciplines which have become independent, like psychology?

Teacher: Other disciplines have developed their own methods and ways of experimentation. They have become so specialized that they had to become independent. They can thrive on their own due to the richness of their subject, and they can also afford to be highly specialized.

In the case of ethics, there are many broad questions that constantly come up, and in addition ethics has its own subdisciplines. At the same time, ethics maintains the kind of speculative approach that characterizes philosophy in general, and hence it remains a part of philosophy. Equally, it remains abstract or theoretical in the sense that it does not have an immediate empirical basis, another reason for it to remain a part of philosophy. Ethics is rooted in certain central debates within philosophy, such as the question of human nature and the ideal rules of conduct among human beings. In that sense, it remains firmly a discipline within the humanities as well as philosophy.

Student: If ethics is a part of philosophy, what role does it play within philosophy?

Teacher: Philosophy reflects on all aspects of reality and the disciplines of human knowledge, and ethics reflects on the relations among human beings, in other words, the way in which we treat and should treat others. More recently, it has also come to include the way in which we relate to other species or even the natural environment. However, the main themes within ethics remain the relations among human beings. In the case of virtue, this can also include the way in which we treat ourselves, as we shall see. Some virtues concern the question of self-control. In any case, ethics appears to be an almost purely human affair, at least in the sense that it describes and seeks to improve human behavior and conduct.

Student: Does that mean that ethics treats essentially of the relations among human beings?

Teacher: Yes, although it can include the way in which we treat not just other human beings but also the rest of nature, such as other sentient beings and species, namely other animals, and also plants. These fields of ethical studies are called environmental ethics and animal ethics. Ethics tends to describe human conduct towards, primarily but not exclusively, other human beings.

Student: And it is a purely speculative reflection?

Teacher: Ethics consists essentially in a speculative reflection, but it can interact with other disciplines, some of which are more practical or experimental, in particular psychology. For instance, moral psychology analyzes the development of the moral character of human beings and the moral characteristics and behavior of human beings from an experimental perspective. More generally, it studies the intersection of psychology, as an experimental discipline, with ethics and moral behavior. Naturally, this scientific reflection follows the scientific method, which entails formulating a hypothesis and the testing of that hypothesis, and not merely an informal empirical observation that each of us can carry out. Ethics is also an interdisciplinary field in itself, given its strong links with other disciplines which were part of philosophy, such as politics and psychology. For Aristotle and Plato before him, these links are very clear, as we shall see.

Student: Ethics then interacts with the various sciences.

Teacher: Yes, in the case of bioethics, and also in the case of neuroethics.

Student: Does neuroethics examine the biological underpinnings of human action as studied in ethics?

Teacher: That is one of the aspects of neuroethics, but it also analyzes the ethical implications of the scientific study of the brain, namely neuroscience, and in that sense neuroethics is closely related to bioethics.

Student: However, we have emphasized the fact that if our ethical decisions were purely based on biology, this would cause many problems and would likely lead to the end of ethics as an autonomous discipline.

Teacher: That is correct, especially if we think of our decisions as biologically or naturally determined. Freedom, particularly the reality of free will, as we shall see, is an essential aspect of ethical theory. Even some determinist philosophers, like Spinoza, emphasize the significance of freedom as a foundation for ethical theory. Natural or scientific determinism can be considered one of the threats to moral action and, more broadly speaking, ethical theory.

Student: From a philosophical point of view, there are various practical ramifications of ethics?

Teacher: Ethics has been traditionally conceived as part of practical philosophy, as opposed to speculative or theoretical philosophy, which are purely descriptive. Ethics entails human knowledge but also concerns human action. In this sense, it can even be considered as practical philosophy from more than just one point of view. It is about action and it can describe the kinds of human interactions, but it can also recommend or prescribe correct action. It has been said that ethics is not about describing reality and stating how things are, but how they ought to be, in reference to human action.

Student: Is ethics primarily descriptive, or can it prescribe the kind of desired human conduct? Should ethics limit itself to describing human behavior, or should it prescribe the correct course of action?

Teacher: Ethics can do both. Ethics concerns and describes the way in which we deal with each other, but it is difficult to imagine ethics simply describing human behavior. Since the question of good and evil, and particularly moral good and evil, is an essential part of ethics, it is difficult for ethics to analyze human action without, at the same, time, describing correct human action. In that sense, ethics is prescriptive or normative, and not just descriptive. If we describe good conduct, we also expect that type of conduct to become the norm.

Student: Is it not the case that different philosophers have different approaches to ethical theory and the way in which it should be applied?

Teacher: Naturally, different philosophers have different views on moral value and what the right course of action should be.

Moreover, ethics can be more prescriptive than descriptive, depending on one's approach. This question is not unrelated to the connection between ethics and other philosophical disciplines. It can depend, more specifically, on the way in which we view the connection between ethics and metaphysics or philosophical anthropology. Ethics can begin by analyzing human nature in order to build an ethical theory based on human nature as a whole, which is the way followed by Aristotle, who is considered a naturalist in this sense.

Student: Does this mean that Aristotle builds his ethical theory on his view of human nature?

Teacher: Yes, and he sees ethics as a prolongation or perfecting of human nature. In the same way that the crafts perfect nature, and medicine for instance perfects human physical nature, so ethics perfects human character. We naturally have the potential to be good, but there has to be a conscious effort on the part of the agent to develop that potential goodness. In the same way, the virtues can be developed through a certain effort which is described in the discipline of ethics.

Student: Then moral character is a natural continuation of human nature?

Teacher: Yes, and all the aspects which belong to human nature are taken into account in that description. The emotions, for instance, are part of human nature as a whole, and they must be taken account of and participate in the process of acquiring and perfecting the virtues, according to the naturalist approach. It is important to emphasize that although for Aristotle, and other philosophers, ethical theory must be based on human nature, it is not totally determined by it, since we have freedom of action. Other philosophers may think of human nature as not entirely good, in which case ethics and virtue would assume a corrective aspect, rather than highlighting the ability to enhance human nature.

Student: With regard to human nature and its different elements, are other philosophers not so keen on integrating the emotions into their vision of ethics?

Teacher: Many philosophers acknowledge the emotions as an integral part of human nature, but not all see them in a positive light. In the modern period, a philosopher like Kant bases ethics on absolute universal principles which disregard some aspects of human nature, such as the emotions, which should not be involved when it comes to making decisions on moral matters. Before him, Hume does not believe that one can proceed to describing how matters ought to be from simply observing them, particularly when it comes to human action. The connection between ethics and the other philosophical disciplines is complex. Nevertheless, for Hume virtue is a subjective matter rather than something based on ascertainable principles. Before Kant and Hume, Spinoza studies the emotions and advocates their control through reason, which can turn their action to good effect. Understanding the emotions helps us to neutralize any negative aspect which they may present. Other philosophers view ethics as a development of the emotions and a natural sense of the good, such as Shaftesbury.

Student: In addition to the question of human nature and how it is conceived, you also mentioned the connection between ethics and epistemology.

Teacher: Ethics tends to be articulated with other philosophical disciplines, in particular metaphysics and epistemology, although it constitutes its own very special domain within philosophy, with its own branches. We also find a correspondence between metaphysical and epistemological theories, on the one hand, and ethical theories, on the other, in particular authors. Plato has his own theory of the virtues and his virtue ethics, which was influenced by Socrates, who identified virtue with knowledge. For Plato, the association of virtue with knowledge is very strong. In Aristotle, empirical observation plays a greater role, and this is also observable in his ethics. While for Socrates, and perhaps also Plato, ethics, with its focus on virtue, is, at least potentially, an exact science or kind of knowledge, for Aristotle it is not as precise and is based more on custom than on purely theoretical knowledge. The link between ethics and epistemology can determine the way in which we view ethics, whether as an accurate science, or as a rough guiding principle of action.

In addition, Aristotle distinguishes between ethics as a specific kind of human action, and the practical arts or skills. The latter result in a product, while ethics deals with action that does not produce an object, although it has important consequences. It appears that the comparison between practical skills and ethical action in Aristotle is based on his emphasis on habit and the need to practice the virtues in order to become good at them.

Student: This practical aspect of ethics seems very important to me, and the way in which ethics can prescribe correct action.

Teacher: Yes, and this can be the subject of metaethics, which studies, among other themes, whether ethics is descriptive of real value and what is good or bad, and whether questions about value are subjective rather than objective. These are some of the broader questions pertaining to ethics and the study of ethics.

Student: These are very important questions, since they seem to ground ethics. I understand the significance of the strong link between ethics and metaethics, and also between ethics and other philosophical disciplines.

Teacher: We cannot disregard those connections. Both Aristotle and Aquinas, for instance, implicitly and explicitly establish links between ethics on the one hand, and metaphysics and epistemology on the other. Aristotle bases his ethics on a certain understanding of human nature, as we have seen. He proceeds from the perceived way of being human to the way that human nature is best developed. Aquinas is perhaps even more systematic and explicit in the way he bases his ethics on certain metaphysical and epistemological presuppositions. In his account, the intellect, which studies reality, has the truth as its object, but the faculty which ultimately leads to action is the will, which he defines as rational appetite. While truth, which describes reality, is the object of the intellect, and that which the intellect seeks, the good is the object of the will. However, in a certain way, the good and the true are interchangeable. Together with the one and the existent, the good and the true constitute the main transcendentals or the most general categories of existence that we can contemplate, according to medieval philosophers.

Student: I understand that being or existence can also be conceived as something good and true, and one. These general concepts are an important foundation for ethics.

Teacher: Yes, and we will return to those topics in the course of our discussion.

Student: What does the term 'ethics' mean specifically, and how does it relate to morals?

Teacher: The term 'ethos' in Greek means character and also custom. In contemporary English, it can refer to one's character. In the same way, moral comes from 'mos' in Latin, which also means custom and habit, but can be used to discuss virtue. In his *Commentary on the Nicomachean Ethics*, Aquinas distinguishes between 'ethos' and 'ēthos' (with an ēta), the former pertaining to virtue and the later to habit. For Aquinas, this term indicates a natural inclination to perform an action. Naturally, it points to the customary way in which we deal with other people, or the habits and customs of different people. For Aquinas, this custom becomes a second nature. Naturally, there is a correct way of dealing with others, in order to produce harmony in human societies, in addition to perfecting individual human nature, which is the basis and the goal of ethics.

Student: Yes, clearly ethics cannot be purely descriptive, but must play a central role in setting the standards for the best course of human action. If it is natural for human beings to live in communities, as many philosophers stress, then getting along with other human beings must be natural and good at the same time. Then ethics must describe the best way to interact with others, which is also the most natural way.

Teacher: That is correct, and apart from the question of good and evil, ethics also discusses the question of right and wrong, which has an even more prescriptive or normative connotation.

Student: With regard to terminology, is there a distinction between the two terms, 'ethics' and 'morals' or 'morality'?

Teacher: Ethics is sometimes associated with a particular code of conduct; sometimes morals is associated with a particular code of conduct, for instance when we speak of 'Victorian morality', which refers to a particular concept of morality at a particular time and place. Ethics can at times be viewed as more general and merely descriptive, whereas morals seems more specific of certain countries or regions, but the two terms can be interchangeable in this way. Moreover, each of these terms can refer to individual behavior or to the customs of a group of people.

Student: Somehow the term morals seems more specific, perhaps understood specifically as morality.

Teacher: That is correct. When we refer to the philosophical discipline dealing with human behavior and codes of conduct, we tend to speak of ethics, which seems to be a more abstract term. However, ethics and morals can be interchangeable. Morality need not refer to a particular period of time or set of practical rules. For instance, we speak of the British moralists who focused on ethical questions, and had definite views on those issues. However, they were also writing on ethical questions, broadly conceived. One of the terms can be more widely used than the other, at particular times or for specific philosophers.

Student: Is there a particular way in which the several disciplines within ethics are structured?

Teacher: We have seen that ethics intersects with other philosophical disciplines, such as metaphysics, epistemology and philosophical anthropology, and the different sciences. Within ethics, we can think of theoretical or applied ethics. Metaethics studies the principles and basic concepts within ethics. Within theoretical ethics we can consider theories based on the notions of virtue, duty and utility.

2. The Presuppositions of Ethics

2.1. Voluntariness

Student: Are there certain presuppositions which one must take into account when discussing ethics?

Teacher: Yes, these are ethical presuppositions, a kind of first principles or grounding principles of ethics. As we have seen, ethics or morality tends to be prescriptive, or normative. As part of the presuppositions of ethics, we can find an identification, in some cases, between what the case should be and what we must take the case to be. In other words, an ethical ideal is the starting principle and also the goal of ethics.

Student: Are there specific examples of these presuppositions or principles of ethics?

Teacher: Perhaps the most important of all is freedom of action, and the related question of free will, or free will in alliance with and as underpinning freedom of action. Aristotle, and Aristotelian philosophers, state that ethics is about what is up to us. Some scholars hold that one cannot find a concept of will as a separate faculty of the soul in Aristotle, and that it would emerge and become developed in the Middle Ages, being particularly clear in Saint Augustine. However, the concept of 'up to us', and wish or appetite, is very clear in Aristotle. In the theoretical sciences, the mind or the intellect simply apprehends reality. It is active in this process but in the process of knowing it does not change what it apprehends. However, when it comes to ethics, the process of deciding and acting is analyzed in so far as human beings can choose different courses of action, and 'choice' is very much part of Aristotle's ethics. Ethics is about the things that can be changed and that we can change. In addition, there is a connection between knowledge and action in the ethical analysis of human action.

Student: This specific aspect of ethics sets it apart from other disciplines of knowledge?

Teacher: Yes, the ability of putting ethical norms into practice is very important. In that sense we find several ramifications of ethics for legal theory and other domains of human action. For instance, there is a clear link between freedom and responsibility. It is only when we have the freedom to act and the action is up to us that we may be held responsible for it.

Student: We have seen that different philosophers view the connection between ethics and epistemology in different ways, which has implications for the role of emotion or reason in acting.

Teacher: Yes, although the connection between ethics and epistemology is usually present. Some philosophers may take a non-cognitivist approach, which means for instance that moral beliefs are not considered to be true or false, and thus morality or ethics is not necessarily based on knowledge. Rather, it is based on emotions. Hume, for instance, does not link the virtues to objective values, but to emotions and that which has the capacity to affect and please us.

Student: This means that we can find rationalism in ethics, or emotivism as opposed to that rationalism? Perhaps that has implications for the way in which we view voluntary action.

Teacher: That is right; different philosophers have differing views on the role of knowledge within ethics, broadly speaking. Some say that ethical action is based on emotions and others on reason, with its epistemological implications. With regard to the role of emotion, some say that emotion and feelings are part of ethics and of virtue, while others hold that voluntary action is purely a question of rational decision. There is also the link between voluntary action and freedom. Free will is considered to exist only in rational beings, to the exclusion, for instance, of animals.

Student: The role of reason and the emotions within ethics seems to be very complex.

Teacher: We will discuss further the role of emotions and we will see that some philosophers, such as the Stoics, almost completely eliminate the emotions from their conception of virtue. Like Socrates, they hold that reason is the principle of virtuous human action. For Aquinas, both reason and appetite are the principles of human action, not just reason. The Stoics do not believe that the passions can collaborate with reason, rather they are necessarily in disagreement with reason. The will can be more or less influenced by the emotions or non-rational motives.

Student: Even the role of reason and knowledge is complex for philosophers like Plato and Aristotle.

Teacher: Returning to the role of knowledge within ethics, in philosophers such as Plato and Aristotle, the link between knowledge and action is very clear. For Aristotle, virtue is not just about knowledge, as it was for Socrates, but there is a definite dependence of ethics on epistemology. As we will see, Aristotle distinguishes several intellectual virtues as opposed to the moral virtues. According to Socrates, in Plato's dialogues, as long as we have the definition of virtue, which means to know it with complete certainty, we can only act virtuously, for individual virtues and virtue in general. If someone is not virtuous, it is because they do not know the definition of virtue. If someone fails to act courageously when this is required, it is because he or she does not know the definition of courage. There is naturally in Plato a notion of absolute knowledge and ethics that depends directly on that knowledge. Certain or absolute knowledge is also very important for Aristotle, but he holds that ethics does not yield certain knowledge, and for him ethics does not presuppose certain knowledge, unlike other disciplines.

Student: What is the link between reason, knowledge and voluntary action?

Teacher: Even if Aristotle takes account of the emotions and other factors in addition to knowledge, knowledge is central for the understanding of ethics and virtuous action. For instance, voluntary action implies knowledge, as opposed to natural agency or acting through ignorance. One who acts voluntarily must be aware of the particular aspects involved in the action. Forced action is also opposed to voluntary action. Being up to us, voluntary action is also worthy of praise or blame. Clearly, we cannot be blamed or held responsible for something we could not choose or were not aware of. The same applies to natural actions, like scratching one's head, which is an involuntary action or reflex. For Aristotelian philosophers, some natural functions that happen in our bodies, like digestion, are not up to us and thus not within the realm of ethical or virtuous action. If the action is up to us, it means that we are the knowing cause of the action.

In this context, Aristotle describes that which characterizes virtuous action, but these preconditions also pertain to ethical action more generally. At any rate, virtue ethics constitutes ethics for Aristotle. In addition, voluntary action pertains to particular faculties, as we will see later on in greater detail.

Student: Is there a reason why Plato, or rather Socrates, put such an emphasis on knowledge and knowing the definitions of the virtues and of virtue itself, while

Aristotle did not think of ethics in the same way, but also as a question of practice?

Teacher: Aristotle lived in different parts of Greece. He hailed from Macedonia, and he also lived in Athens for several decades. Socrates always lived in Athens, and Plato did travel, but not as much as Aristotle, who was probably influenced in his views on ethics by different customs and types of legal systems in the different parts of the Greek world in which he lived and which he visited.

Student: I understand that Aristotle has a specific view on practical philosophy which is influenced by his experience and his philosophical studies. Does Aristotle have a detailed theory of human action?

Teacher: Yes, and this is found in his major works on ethics, namely the *Nicomachean Ethics*, the *Eudemian Ethics*, and *Magna Moralia*. His main goal is to explain the nature of virtue as that which leads to happiness and constitutes the fulfillment of human nature, in other words, the fulfillment of the human faculties and human nature as a whole.

A central element of virtuous or ethical action is decision or choice, which is a more specific aspect than voluntariness, and involves the state of being rational, or is generally associated with reason. Aristotle states that animals and children may act voluntarily, but not based on decision or choice, given that this involves rational decision and a fully developed rational faculty. One could possibly think of decision or choice as based on wish, appetite or emotion, and thus not necessarily connected with reason or a rational decision, but for Aristotle clearly decision is more specific than voluntary action, which is based on will and involves the use of reason. Later, medieval authors will state that non-rational animals have will, but not free will, which implies decision.

Student: Are there other differences between voluntary action and decision?

Teacher: Aristotle states that we wish for the end but decide on the means leading to the end. We also choose or decide based on that which is within our power, and on that which we find good or bad. We decide on possible things, not things that we cannot change or that cannot be otherwise. According to Aquinas, it is the end which specifies the moral action, and an action can be considered good if the end is good. Typically, the end is a good that is willed by itself.

In addition, Aristotle compares decision and belief. Belief may settle for something we do not know well, but decision is more closely based on knowledge.

Student: Is there a difference between choice and decision?

Teacher: In English we tend to think of choice as implying two possibilities or more, and choosing between them, but decision could also mean that too. Decision, on the other hand, could mean, for instance, to do or not to do something, and reaching a conclusion after a particular consideration, instead of having to choose between two or more options. However, the term used by Aristotle, 'prohairesis', can mean choice or decision, and it can even mean intention, as well as purpose and will. A scholar like Charles Chamberlain prefers to translate it as 'commitment', indicating the process of forming a new desire, a process which involves intention, choice, and decision.

For Aquinas, a good choice implies intending the right end, and employing the right means to the end. It is based on reason, and therefore natural inclination without reason does not constitute choice. This also means that for Aquinas reason must be involved in performing virtuous actions.

Student: And this happens at an individual level?

Teacher: It is clear that Aristotle understands virtue and the practice of virtue as an individual endeavor, which can and should be adopted by most if not all individuals. Nevertheless, his ethics is meant as preliminary to his political theory, and therefore the individual, in her ethical action, is not considered purely in isolation but in connection with other human beings. Moreover, some virtues, such as justice, necessarily imply a relationship with others. As we have mentioned, the universal aspect of virtue is more prominent in Plato's philosophy. One need only have the idea of good, or virtue, in order to be virtuous. Aristotle's approach is much more related to specific circumstances, although he states which preconditions are required for virtuous action to take place. And although virtue can and should be adjusted in accordance with the individual practicing it, it also has general rules.

Student: Regarding the nature of human action, we have concluded that, for Aristotle, voluntary action is not natural action or compelled action, and neither is it action from ignorance.

Teacher: That is true. Voluntary action is up to us, and it implies a conscious choice between good and evil. What is up to us comes from within us and not from outside, and therefore it implies our own agency. In his *Commentary on the* Nicomachean Ethics, Aquinas explain that the voluntary is not just what comes from us, as opposed to immediate external factors. If we follow the sensitive appetite, for instance, we are also being led by external factors, which appeal to our senses.

In addition, doing something willingly means something done with pleasure, as opposed to something which is done by force, which tends to be painful, since it goes against nature. For Aristotle free agency and pleasure are not opposed to ethical and virtuous action. Indeed, the virtuous person acts virtuously with pleasure, and pleasure is a kind of good.

Student: However, surely for Aristotle pleasure is just one of the goods?

Teacher: That is right, and certainly Aristotle thinks of different kinds of pleasure, and physical pleasure is not highly rated by him.

Student: With regard to human nature and the pleasure one takes in acting virtuously, here Aristotle is perhaps assuming a necessary connection between emotion and epistemological aspects pertaining to ethical action, which is not present in other philosophers.

Teacher: That is right. Our emotions or feelings are gratified, resulting in pleasure, as part of voluntary action, but for some philosophers, like the Stoics, emotion can hinder virtuous action and cloud the mind. We will discuss in greater detail the role of emotion in ethical action and its connection with the virtues.

Student: Intention is also an important aspect of voluntary action, correct?

Teacher: That is right. Within ethical and virtuous action, the agent should aim at the good. If the agent acts in the right way by accident, or unintentionally, then this is not considered a virtuous action, and perhaps does not even fall within the realm of ethics. The object of the ethical action is the good, and evil should be avoided, both intentionally and unintentionally. According to Aristotle, voluntary action is a prerequisite for virtuous action, but we could say that voluntary action is, broadly speaking, a requisite for ethical action. Ethics does not really pronounce itself on natural phenomena or compelled action as such.

Student: Voluntary action, the one which falls within the realm of ethics, involves decision?

Teacher: In principle, yes. However, given that voluntary action for Aristotle means that the action comes from within us, and animals also have the power of motion, it is possible, according to Aristotle, to attribute voluntary action to animals.

Student: Does this mean that they have a will?

Teacher: Yes, and later authors also state that non-rational animals have a will, as we have seen, since they act based on some kind of awareness of their surroundings. For instance, the sheep naturally flee the wolf, but this is not a rational process. Choice and decision, then, entail the involvement of reason.

Student: Does Aristotle mention other ways in which reason is part of ethical action?

Teacher: Yes, Aristotle states that deliberation is part of the process of moral action. Again, deliberation is about things that are up to us and that we can change, and not what happens by nature, necessity or chance, which means that deliberation is part of the things that are characteristic of ethical action. Deliberation is about the means to the end rather than the end to be achieved, as Aristotle states in the *Nicomachean Ethics*. Wish is that which aims at the end, and its object is the good.

Student: Aquinas also considers that what is properly considered as human action presupposes the will?

Teacher: Yes, actions that are properly human issue from deliberate will, and the voluntary act is a rational operation. He thinks of the voluntary as issuing from one's own inclination and implying knowledge. Deliberation is about things that can be changed, and that can be changed by us, and therefore are not necessary.

Voluntary action proper implies knowledge of the end. In addition, the will is something that is not compelled, but free to act. He thinks of the will as acting in two ways, simply as wishing and as directing something, for instance in the process that leads up to walking. The will, for Aquinas, is something autonomous, and an intrinsic principle. The will is also an incorporeal power, like the intellect, as he states in the *Summa Theologiae*. According to Aquinas, that which is immaterial has a more universal and far-reaching power, and naturally God is the most powerful and immaterial being. However, in us the will can be moved by the lower appetite, in particular the sensitive appetite, and it can be moved by external things. Aquinas also states that the heavenly bodies do not move the will, that is to say, the human will.

Student: In that sense he would be opposed to a kind of determinism which implies that our action is determined by astrological movements?

Teacher: Yes. The will is an intrinsic principle; it can be moved by external factors, but not by every kind of agent or principle, and not by a material substance like the heavenly bodies.

Student: There is a question regarding the way in which the will and the lower appetites interact.

Teacher: Yes, the body always obeys the will, but the lower appetites or desires have a kind of will or wish of their own and obey in a political or autonomous way. This position is already in Aristotle, for instance in the *Eudemian Ethics*.

Student: I understand that the will is a central human faculty of the soul, and that Aquinas develops the concept of will based on Aristotle's position. What of his debt to Augustine?

Teacher: Yes, Aquinas uses Aristotelian terminology and ideas to develop his own philosophy, but he was also an attentive reader of Augustine, particularly on theological matters. Aquinas has a fully-fledged conception of the will and of free will, while building on Augustine's view of the human will.

Student: With regard to the things which can influence, control or determine the human will, can God move our will?

Teacher: In the *Summa Theologiae*, Aquinas has a very interesting position on that issue. He states that God moves the human will in a universal way, as being the object of our will. Without God moving our will, we are unable to will anything. With regard to particular goods, it is human beings who choose by their reason and will. Aquinas adds that God can move human beings to desire some particular good, by imparting His grace to specific human beings.

Student: And is the good the general object of the will?

Teacher: For Aquinas as for Aristotle, the good is the object of the will, although Aquinas adds that this is ultimately the absolutely good being, namely God. With regard to particular goods, the will also wills the object of the other human powers, such as the object of the intellect. In other words, we may perceive something and then seek to obtain it. In addition, the will wishes to know and attain the truth, and it also desires the goals of the other powers, such as the goals pertaining to the body and anything that keeps us healthy, more specifically, the ends of the body.

Student: According to Aquinas, what would be the obstacles to voluntary action?

Teacher: If one is not physically able to act or complete an action, then the will is prevented from being executed. However, the will is an intrinsic principle, with its own rules, and therefore it cannot be impeded by itself. The outcome of the decision of the will can be impeded, though. In a sense, the will cannot be impeded by itself, no more than a natural action can be impeded unless it runs into an obstacle. However, a voluntary action is closely associated with rational activity, and this is what clearly distinguishes it from natural action. According to Aquinas, the will acts based on an inclination provided by knowledge.

Student: We have previously seen that the close connection between the will and the intellect is characteristic of ancient and medieval philosophy, and that later, philosophers like Descartes and Rousseau think of the will, respectively, as greater than, or separate from, the intellect.

Teacher: Precisely, and this is a kind of rationalism, namely, to think of the intellect as the primary human faculty, and of the will as closely connected to, and dependent on, the intellect, in what constitutes a preference of the intellect over the will. According to these philosophers, a will which is based on knowledge becomes free will.

Student: You mentioned some commonalities between the will and the intellect.

Teacher: Yes, according to Aquinas they are both inner principles, and opposed to violent action, which is something external. Something can move in its own way through nature or through the will, as these are both inner or intrinsic principles. But nature does not presuppose knowledge, in the sense that it is not moved by knowledge, whereas the will is. Violence goes against nature in the case of things without knowledge and it goes against the will in subjects endowed with knowledge, and as such violence can be respectively unnatural or involuntary.

Student: However, involuntariness does not always come from lack of knowledge, correct?

Teacher: Correct. In commenting on Aristotle's position, which states that if something is done through ignorance it is involuntary, Aquinas, in the *Summa Theologiae*, argues that there are different kinds of involuntariness and ignorance. There is willful ignorance, if one does not take into account what one should take into account, due to a passion or a habit, or if one neglects to acquire the necessary knowledge. He gives the example of the principles of the law, which one should know. Not to know them is voluntary and arises from negligence, and it is blameworthy. This is not direct involuntariness.

Student: So there is a kind of ignorance that can be avoided?

Teacher: Yes, that is correct. In acting there is involuntariness simply speaking, when one truly does not know, and a different kind of involuntariness, when there are circumstances that one ought to know. It is very important to be aware of the circumstances. Aquinas thinks of the circumstances as important and attaching to the act. The circumstances stand to the act as accidents to the substance, and the circumstances may pertain to the act itself, and the way it is done, or to the person, such as the place and condition of the agent.

Student: You have mentioned that for Aquinas the will is a rational appetite.

Teacher: Yes, and appetite is a general term which indicates a power moving other powers or faculties of the soul towards their ends. In that sense, the virtues for Aristotle correspond to the different parts of the soul, as directed by reason.

Moreover, for Aquinas there are several aspects associated with the will. For instance, intention is an act of the will as pertaining to the end. In relation to the end, the will is volition, as it wishes for the end; as enjoyment, it rests in the end, and as intention, it considers the end as the term of something.

Student: Is choice an act of the will?

Teacher: Following Aristotle, Aquinas states that choice is a desire for those things which are in our power, that is to say, which are up to us. He also says that choice is an act of the appetitive power, and that it belongs to the will. Choice is therefore more specific than will. Choice is one of the acts of the will and it concerns the means, while volition concerns the end. Naturally, choice is of that which is possible, not the impossible. With regard to the connection of the will with the intellect, the latter proposes the object of the will, which causes the external action. Choice is an act of the rational power, and the will is a rational power, a rational appetite. Another act of reason and of the will is counsel, through which a decision is made concerning particular contingent things involved in an action. Consent is another element, belonging to the higher reason, and in it the intellect is moved by the will.

Student: I understand that Aquinas describes the mechanism of voluntary action before discussing virtue. How are these different elements of the action related?

Teacher: In the *Summa Theologiae*, Aquinas states that the order of action consists in apprehending the end, then desiring the end, followed by counsel concerning the means and the desire of the means. The appetite tends towards the last end, and counsel concerns the means to the end. The end is some good that is desired.

Student: Does Aristotle comment on the kind of good that is wished for?

Teacher: This is an important aspect. In the same way that before speaking of virtue it is important to discuss the principles of ethics and the presuppositions or the preconditions of virtue, we must establish the end of ethics and of virtue, so the beginning and the end of ethics and virtue.

2.2. The Conception of the Good and Happiness

Student: Aristotle states that the goal of human action or ethical action is the good. Is the good the same for everyone?

Teacher: Aristotle states that the good is the end for everyone, but the end could also be the apparent good. Some think that the good is pleasure; this could be physical pleasure, and Aristotle does not hold this to be the truly good. Sometimes people choose an apparent rather than a real good as goal.

Student: Naturally, the good is a very complex topic. It seems that the good as the intended goal of ethical action can be seen as a precondition of virtue, but at the same time it is the final cause or the goal of ethical action.

Teacher: That is right. Ethical action implies intention, and the intended goal is the good. We could discuss whether the good is one or many, and whether it is the same for different people, because the good and the end can be several things. Plato and Aristotle differ on the nature of the 'good'. For Plato, it tends to be one thing, or form, possibly the most important form, as described by Plato in the *Republic*. Plato thinks of the good as one, and Aristotle thinks of it as many things. For Plato, the good is the same regardless of the person.

For Aristotle, there are different kinds of goods, but some are more important than others. Generally speaking, the good is sought by everything; it is the end goal or the typical final cause itself. The end that is sought is always something good. Some ends are subordinate to others. We know that the good is like the final cause because Aristotle does not wish to see an infinite regress, or rather infinite progress, of the final cause. We may want to attain something for the sake of something else. For instance, we may wish to be healthy in order to attain physical well-being. But ultimately there must be a final good. Within a political context, we can also think of the good of the individual and the good of the community, and how one contributes to the other. In addition, each science has its own good and goal. For human beings, the end is to live well, and for ancient and medieval philosophers, this is typically the activity of the soul, which is virtue.

Student: Is it possible to think of the individual good as the moral or ethical goal, and the common good as the political goal?

Teacher: Yes, even if the ethical dimension seems to be more general than the political. Ethics pertains to human relations in general and so, in a certain sense, it embraces the political. More specifically, ethics deals with the behavior of the individual, and individual human relations, whereas politics discusses human communities and the organization of those communities. For Aristotle, both ethics and politics are part of practical philosophy. Ethics is the starting point for the discussion of politics.

Student: In that sense, politics would be the goal of ethics?

Teacher: Yes, which means that politics would be more important than ethics and even comprise the treatment of ethics. This is because the common good, possibly because it comprises a greater number of people, is more important than the individual good and individual ethical behavior, according to ancient and medieval philosophers. At the same time, there is no discussion of politics and the political community without the treatment of the individual and of human nature. We always encounter this tension between the individual and the universal, but a separate treatment of ethics is fully warranted, since the universal only exists based on the individual, at least for Aristotle.

Student: I understand that ethics and the discussion of human nature should be our starting point, and this is the approach that we have been taking. Returning to the goal of ethics, the good is not solely the subject of ethics?

Teacher: No, it is also analyzed in other disciplines, like metaphysics. Each discipline has its own good which is its goal. For instance, the goal of medicine is maintaining and restoring health in human beings. In speaking of the ends as goals, and as goods, Aristotle states that some are more complete than others.

Student: Does that mean that each good is a goal?

Teacher: Yes, but we should also keep in mind that there are incomplete and complete kinds of goods, and the incomplete ones require a further good or further goods.

Student: Then some goods are not the end, or not the ultimate end, but the means to the end?

Teacher: That is correct; the good can also mean something useful, which naturally is not the end in itself. The good as useful is an incomplete good. Nowadays there is a tendency to think of the useful as the most important thing and as a good in itself, but in fact something useful is a means to an end. If an end is self-sufficient, and does not require something else, it is complete. The useful is an incomplete kind of good.

Student: What does Aristotle consider to be the complete or ultimate good?

Teacher: He identifies this complete good with happiness, because we do not choose happiness for the sake of anything else. We can never say that we want to be happy as a means to some further end, or for the sake of something else.

Student: However, even if the goal is the same, perhaps there are different ways to attain happiness?

Teacher: That is right, and this means that people have different conceptions of happiness. Some identify it with pleasure, some with honor, and others with virtue. Aristotle holds that happiness is made up of many goods.

Student: What are these goods?

Teacher: He states that we can distinguish between the goods of the soul, the goods of the body, and external goods. Happiness requires all of these, including external goods. For Aristotle, happiness is the activity of the good soul, but happiness requires more than virtue, which is the typical good of the soul, as he states in the *Nicomachean Ethics*.

Student: What is the difference between these kinds of goods?

Teacher: The goods of the soul are the virtues, which include the intellectual or theoretical virtues as well as the moral virtues, as we will see. Knowledge is a good of the soul, for instance, but so are the moral virtues, or virtues of character, such as justice or courage. And naturally, the virtues must be in the soul or the mind — they cannot exist elsewhere, as something immaterial. Moreover, each science seeks a particular good and end, as we have seen.

Student: That makes sense, since they are specifically human, for Aristotle, and for other philosophers. What about the other goods?

Teacher: The other goods are easier to explain. The goods of the body are typically health or well-being. External goods are things like wealth and honor and reputation.

Student: Does Aristotle privilege some of these goods?

Teacher: Aristotle favors the goods of the soul. The good is something which we have the potential to obtain, and which we must strive to obtain. Aristotle says that the virtuous person is a standard in choosing and aiming at the true good. Perhaps Aristotle inherits from Plato the idea that the virtues and the good qualities of the soul are immortal and stable, unlike other kinds of goods, and are therefore more valuable.

Student: That sounds right, since the body itself is not considered by Plato to be incorruptible or immortal in the way that the soul is, as we know from the *Phaedo*.

Teacher: Yes, and the external goods can be even more fleeting. There is also the question of the ease of obtaining or maintaining those goods. We cannot truly control our reputation, and even keeping in good health may not be easy, but we have more control over whether we decide to be virtuous or not.

Student: This was also an important point for the Stoics, was it not?

Teacher: Yes, these are related issues that the Stoics took up. According to the Stoics, virtue was the only true good, and it alone produced happiness. The other goods are considered indifferents, and they can be advantageous, but are not really good, or true goods.

Student: Why does Aristotle include goods such as friends and family as necessary for happiness?

Teacher: He believes that we are social animals and are not complete unless we live in society, and family is also part of society. This also means that we are not completely fulfilled except in society, and do not attain the full human potential in isolation; therefore we need family and friends in order to be happy. In addition, some virtues are directed at others, like justice, and therefore it is difficult to practice them if we live in isolation.

Student: Does this mean that Aristotle privileges the active life over the contemplative life?

Teacher: As in Plato, we find in Aristotle a tension between these two kinds of life, and it is unclear which of the two is worthier and more fulfilling. In the *Nicomachean Ethics*, Aristotle mentions the three types of life: the life of pleasure, the political life, and the life of study. Aristotle does not think highly of the life of pleasure, which he appears to identify with physical pleasure, as this is not truly different from a life that other animals live. This kind of life seems to disregard the rational function of human beings. Those who follow this kind of life think of pleasure as the ultimate goal. Then comes the political life, and those who pursue it think of honor as the ultimate goal in life. The problem is that this kind of life does not depend so much on the subject of political action but on those around him or her. Whether we are honored or not is not up to us. Naturally we may act in ways that seek recognition from others for our good deeds, but it is up to others to honor us or not. And in any case honor tends to attach to those who are virtuous, which means that virtue is a higher goal than honor.

Student: In the case of honor, it seems that an active political life is required.

Teacher: That is right. The contemplative life is very important, and as we shall see, it relies on the use of the intellectual virtues. Within the domain of the virtues, there is a distinction between the theoretical or intellectual virtues, and the moral virtues, which are the virtues of character. Within Plato's dialogues, we find Socrates in the *Apology* stating that the philosopher, who inquires into the nature of virtue more than anything else, should lead a quiet life and pursue his activities in private, since justice is at odds with politics in the sense that it cannot be pursued by one who enters politics. However, in the *Republic*, the philosopher is urged to leave his private activities and become actively involved in politics. Indeed, he should not just become involved in politics, but should become the ruler, for, given his theoretical and practical virtues, he is the most qualified of all citizens to rule the city and the polity. We will learn more about the connection between the practical and the intellectual or theoretical virtues later.

Student: Are there other ways in which external goods can help us become happy?

Teacher: There are certain kinds of virtue, like generosity, which require the material means to exercise that particular virtue. We have greater power to help others, generally speaking, if we have the means to do it. However, we can think of ways of helping others that do not require external goods. We can offer our time and dedication, which is different from material means that derive from wealth. Having friends can also make it easier to help others. Political power is an external good, and it is not as important as virtue, but again, according to Aristotle, it can help us to exercise our virtues and help others in a general way.

Student: Are there other aspects of the happy life that we should take into account in this context, in addition to external goods?

Teacher: Aristotle compares the relative merits of capacity and activity, and thinks of happiness in terms of activity rather than capacity.

Student: Is there a particular motive that explains why Aristotle thinks of activity as more important than capacity?

Teacher: We need to be active in order to fulfill our human nature, and being active by exercising the virtues, intellectual or moral, is the way to lead a fulfilling life and to perform our function in society. Fulfilling the virtues at a political, communal level will create the conditions for the practice of virtue by all individuals within society, laying the foundations for individual and also communal virtuous practice. Both virtue and happiness imply activity.

Student: And both virtue and happiness are ends in themselves, since happiness is an ultimate goal, and virtue too is not really a means to an end, but an end in itself.

Teacher: Virtue is the goal of ethical life, but it cannot be grasped without understanding those who practice virtue; in other words, we learn about virtue from observing virtuous people. For Aristotle, the measure of virtue and an ideal ethical life is the virtuous person, but he also thinks of the goods of the soul, like virtue and happiness, as the most important kinds of good.

    For the Stoics it is clear that we can decide whether to be virtuous or not, but we cannot decide whether we will be wealthy, for instance. If virtue intrinsically entails happiness or is the same as happiness, and we can decide whether to be virtuous, then we can decide, according to the Stoics, whether to be happy or not. In other words, it is up to us to be happy or not, simply by choosing to be virtuous.

Student: Yes, the question of the end as the ultimate goal seems quite complex but also very important in this context.

Teacher: Since we are discussing the different kinds of goods, and which ones are instrumental and which are final and complete, it is important to stress that this is a question about the end goal of human life.

We have seen how ethics is something which is specifically about human relations and how they ideally should be. All disciplines of knowledge contain a human element in the sense of being developed by human beings. In addition, some disciplines study different aspects of human society, like sociology and anthropology. Ethics, in its analysis of human relations, has a strong normative or prescriptive aspect and is about the end goal of human life.

Student: And ethics naturally includes not only the way in which we treat others, and ourselves, but also the goal of human life.

Teacher: Yes, ethics is about the way in which we treat others and ourselves, and we can say more broadly that it is about the goal of human life.

Student: And that goal is the good, but we could say that this can mean more than one thing?

Teacher: That is right. The goal is the good and the specifically human goal appears to be happiness.

Student: The goods, as the object of the will, can be one or many?

Teacher: Yes. We have seen that for the Stoics there is only one good, which is virtue or happiness, and these are identical. Aristotle includes other goals, and also external goods, as important goals to obtain, even for the practice of virtue. There are similarities between Aristotle and the Stoics in the way that virtue is the highest good, alongside happiness.

In addition, the similarities between the Stoics and Socrates are patent, and it is clear that the Stoics were inspired by Socrates in their conception of virtue. As we know, Socrates influenced different schools of thought in ancient Greece.

Student: Other philosophers also consider the question of the human goal and the ultimate good.

Teacher: Yes, and Aquinas later states that the object of the will is the good, and that it is a goal of the will, and the goal of human beings, too. We can think of certain goods as the means to an end, and in other words the good as the useful, but the good itself is the end and not the means to an end, as we have seen.

Student: Does Aquinas explain the connection between the good and human action?

Teacher: In the *Summa Theologiae*, Aquinas states that the goodness of human actions can be discerned in terms of genus (the action itself), species (the object of the action), the circumstances, and the end. In turn, the goodness of the will depends on its being subject to reason, and it also depends on its adherence to the eternal law, that is to say, divine law.

Student: That makes sense in Aquinas, if everything coming from God is superior to what comes from us.

Teacher: Exactly, and the measure of human goodness is divine goodness. We must align ourselves and our actions with divine law, and for him even natural law ultimately comes from divine law.

Student: This means that human will should follow reason, and ultimately divine reason?

Teacher: Yes, exactly. An evil will is the one which is at variance with reason. For him, an action is good or evil depending on free will, and in so far as it is voluntary.

Student: That means that nonvoluntary action, or an action that does not involve free will, cannot be considered good or evil?

Teacher: It cannot be considered good or evil from a moral point of view. In order for it to be considered in that way, the action must be in the agent's power. Yet again, if ignorance is not involuntary, if someone does not wish to know, there can be blame attributed to the agent. The will is good based on the good aimed at, which is for the sake of the good itself, and it should be aligned with the divine will.

Student: Does that mean that an evil will is the one which goes against the divine will?

Teacher: Yes, and with regard to the good, the common good is also identified with the divine good, and as the ultimate good established by God.

Student: And what is the connection between the particular good and the common good?

Teacher: Aquinas holds that we should keep in mind the common good even in pursuing our own particular good. One is only justified in seeking a particular good if the common good is ultimately one's goal.

Student: Does Aquinas also state that everything must be good in the action that is performed?

Teacher: Yes, the intention has to be good, but the end is chosen by the will, while the circumstances come under the power of reason.

Student: And the outcome should also be good?

Teacher: According to Aquinas, the consequences do not bear on whether an action is good or evil. If funds given to charity are misused, this does not mean that the action in itself was bad, and if one suffers wrongdoing it does not mean that the wrongdoer is excused. In the same way, a thing should not be judged on the basis of its accidents.

Student: Aquinas also discusses many things pertaining to virtue before discussing virtue proper, then?

Teacher: In the *Summa Theologiae*, Aquinas follows a certain sequence before discussing the virtues: namely, he describes first the end, which is happiness, then the nature of the will and voluntary actions, then the passions, and habit, before proceeding to a detailed discussion of the various virtues, including the moral, the intellectual and the theological virtues.

Student: Perhaps we could discuss further the goal of virtue, before discussing virtue in greater detail. We notice a close connection between virtue, the good, happiness and the end goal. It seems that the goal of human living is both the good and happiness, and also virtue, since virtue is not a means to an end. Happiness is a good, then?

Teacher: Yes, and naturally this is a very important topic. Aristotle says many important things about happiness and happiness appears to be the objective of a virtuous life, and identical also with a virtuous life, although Aristotle holds that virtue alone is not sufficient for obtaining happiness. He holds that happiness consists in leading a virtuous life; he identifies happiness with activity and also the fulfillment of human nature, which is typically rational. Being virtuous and good and happy means to fulfill the function of being human. But there are several ways to do this. We have a certain function or typical activity, and Aristotle identifies this with reason and thinking. In addition, happiness consists more in an activity than in staying idle. Although other aspects of human life are important, like sensing and moving, it is reasoning that distinguishes us from other animals.

Student: Happiness seems then to be the central goal of human life.

Teacher: Yes, and for Aristotle it is not an easy goal to attain, because we need several kinds of goods.

Student: But naturally, when it comes to happiness, which everyone seeks, the most important factors must be the virtues, and ethical action?

Teacher: That is true. It is clear from Aristotle's ethical works that virtue is the most important of the different kinds of goods, because it is the good of the soul, and the soul and its activity are the most important aspect contributing to happiness. Happiness means to fulfill human nature, as we have seen, and this means to live in a specifically human way, which is tantamount to rational contemplation. However, the other virtues, not just intellectual but also moral, are included in the process of attaining happiness, as well as the goods of the body and external goods.

Student: For Aristotle, then, the external goods and the goods of the body are means to the ultimate end, which is happiness?

Teacher: Yes, those are clearly subordinate goods.

Student: And with regard to happiness, there are different conceptions, but we have seen that for Aristotle it requires several goods and consists in the fulfillment of human nature through virtuous activity. However, human nature could imply several kinds of activity?

Teacher: It is clear that Aristotle thinks of happiness as consisting primarily of virtuous activity. He tackles the question of happiness, which he considers the end goal of human life, in his ethics, and his ethics is centered on virtue. So clearly, there is a very strong, inextricable connection between virtue and happiness. One might think of typically human activity as practicing a craft, like shoemaking. However, Aristotle's ethical works, which deal with happiness, specifically distinguish the kind of human action that does not produce an object but has its goal in itself, as ethical activity which leads to happiness. Therefore, the production of objects does not appear to be directly associated with happiness.

Student: Nevertheless, happiness as virtuous activity could have a more practical or theoretical character, right? Does it necessarily mean dealing with other people?

Teacher: Yes, the two aspects of virtue, practical and theoretical, are patent in Aristotle. We have already seen that there is a tension between the respective value of the contemplative versus the political life, both in Plato and in Aristotle. With regard to happiness, the same applies. One might think that happiness consists in interacting with other people, in a good and virtuous way. This could be the height of happiness, and for this we require the moral virtues.

Student: Aristotle also considers the intellectual virtues as part of his schema of human virtues.

Teacher: Exactly, and the intellectual virtues do not necessarily involve interacting with other people. Towards the end of the *Nicomachean Ethics*, Aristotle tends to think of true happiness as contemplative activity.

Student: It seems that we are faced with the same dilemma as with the distinction between contemplation and politics, as to which is the more valuable activity.

Teacher: That is right. However, we can find a link between the two kinds of virtue in the way the moral virtues require the intellectual virtues, or at least wisdom or prudence. And since we live in society, the moral virtues are also required. Plato and Aristotle, and later philosophers inspired by them, such as Alfarabi, hold that human beings naturally live in society, rather than in isolation. With regard to the two kinds of virtue, moral and intellectual, they inform one another, as we shall see.

Student: Is there a distinction between intellectual and moral virtues in Plato?

Teacher: Naturally, Plato's works are not as systematic as Aristotle's, as we have received them, consisting mainly in dialogues where various concepts are discussed and evaluated. The various virtues are analyzed in Plato's dialogues. The *Meno* examines virtue in general, but as we know, a definition is not reached. However, if we think of the Aristotelian distinction between intellectual and moral virtues, we observe that Plato discusses those virtues. He treats virtues like temperance, courage and justice, which Aristotle considers to be moral virtues, but he also mentions wisdom or prudence, which Aristotle considers to be an intellectual virtue. However, perhaps Plato does not make such a distinction, and the virtues are all related to knowledge and also practical action. For Plato, even the virtues that Aristotle considers to be the moral virtues are closely dependent on knowledge, in a theory that is inspired by Socrates. In fact, for Socrates, and to some extent for Plato, virtue is knowledge. This does not mean that all knowledge is a kind of virtue, such as for instance mathematical knowledge, but virtue is always about knowledge, in the sense that virtue is always some kind of knowledge.

Student: If we pursue the theme of virtue as a goal, or the goals of virtue, happiness appears to constitute that goal, as we have seen. Aristotle also studies the way to attain happiness, does he not?

Teacher: He does. We have seen that according to Aristotle different people have different conceptions of happiness, or activities which they identify with happiness or otherwise lead to happiness. For Aristotle, as we have seen, it is not possible for one to be happy without being virtuous. In addition, Aristotle maintains that happiness is not amusement or entertainment, but a more permanent state, even if he does not disregard the merits of amusement. He thinks of amusement as important for relaxation, and as a preparation for activity. In that sense, it is very important.

Again, although happiness is the goal of virtuous life, and can in some ways be identified with the virtuous life, it is examined by Aristotle in the *Nicomachean Ethics* before he goes into details regarding the virtues, as well as at the end of that work. Happiness is the goal and the motivation for the virtues. It is the goal but it is also the starting point of the discussion about the virtues. It is a precondition for discussing the virtues, as well as the purpose of the virtues. Aristotle does not believe that happiness is attained by fortune or chance.

Student: Is that because happiness is closely associated with virtue, and virtue is something that does not happen to us, but is cultivated by us?

Teacher: That is right. Some of the characteristics of virtue and ethical action also apply to happiness. Happiness is a human activity centered on the soul, and it is not possible to be happy without the virtues, since we are not fulfilling what is typically human. In addition, he states that happiness is found in activities that are in line with virtue.

Student: Socrates and Plato also believed that it was not possible to be happy without the virtues, right?

Teacher: That is correct. In the Platonic dialogues, Socrates stresses that the person who is not virtuous cannot be happy.

Student: Plato has a different explanation from Aristotle regarding one's need for the virtues in order to be happy, does he not?

Teacher: Exactly. For Aristotle, the need for the virtues implies the fulfillment of human nature, leading to happiness, with the aid of external goods. Aristotle describes the human being as a rational animal, and in his *Politics* he also states that the human being is a political animal. How do we practice those activities? By practicing the intellectual and the moral virtues.

Student: For Plato, virtue is also in the soul?

Teacher: Yes, Plato stresses that virtue is in the soul, like many other philosophers later, but the link between virtue and happiness, alongside the rootedness of the virtues in the soul, is particularly clear in Plato. Virtue is an activity of the soul and for Plato it indicates the harmony of the soul. Someone who does not possess the virtues but rather is overcome by vices does not have a balanced soul, in which the rational element dominates. Naturally, that person has something resembling a diseased soul, and cannot be happy. A happy soul is a soul where virtue and reason, which is the superior part of the soul, reign supreme. Socrates, Plato and Aristotle believe that human beings should live according to their higher abilities, and this means that reason should control the emotions and the body, although they approach this doctrine in somewhat different ways.

Student: I will be curious to know more about the connection between virtue and the emotions, as we proceed with our discussion. In what other ways is virtue linked to the soul?

Teacher: Virtue resides in the human soul. It is a characteristic and an activity of the soul, it is the adornment of the soul, if we choose a more descriptive or poetic language. If we think of human beings as made of body and soul, or body and mind, then virtue is definitely in the soul or the mind.

Student: Those who do not wish to suggest religious connotations can use the term mind.

Teacher: That is right. Mind resembles intellect, but soul is a more complex concept, since it has traditionally been associated with life and life functions such as breathing, motion and thinking. In addition, in the history of philosophy, it is difficult to dissociate the notion of soul from the question of the immortality of the soul, which has religious connotations. Mind is a more neutral concept, but it is not sufficient to help us to understand Aristotle and the way in which he understands virtue. He thinks of the soul as being constituted by various faculties, and some virtues are more closely connected with some faculties than others. This will become clearer later.

Student: It is clear, at any rate, that if we are made up of body and soul, or body and mind, then virtue, and ethical action, are in the mind and not in the body, and virtue issues from the mind rather than the body, even if the body is required to perform some virtuous actions. As have seen in our previous dialogue, concerning the concept of spirit in philosophy, according to Plato and Aristotle the body mostly obeys the soul and depends on the soul in order to be active. And virtue is something that is up to us and is associated with the mind or the intellect, which for Aristotle is one of the parts of the soul.

Teacher: Yes, some parts of the soul are more closely connected with the body, like sensation and sense perception, but it is clear, in any case, that virtue and the soul belong together. In addition, in the history of philosophy some changes can be observed which pertain to the faculties of the soul and its connection with virtue. The will becomes a very important human faculty in the Middle Ages. The intellect and the will soon become the main faculties of the human soul, almost as two sides of the same coin. However, we then see that the intellect and the will do not always agree, and this becomes even more apparent in modern philosophy.

Student: Yes, it could be argued that in Aristotle, will or wish was almost too closely connected with reason to be separate from it. However, both Plato and Aristotle have a notion of free will as that which is up to us, and of the differences between intellect and will. In that sense, it seems that there are different ways to indicate the autonomy we feel when we make decision. We can call it what is up to us, or free will, but it appears to amount to the same thing, basically.

Teacher: I agree, and the articulation of the relationship between intellect and will is particularly obvious when they discuss the virtue of temperance, which implies that the will or desire follows the intellect.

Student: Returning to the concept of happiness, Aristotle also states that happiness is like a divine activity or an activity that is similar to the activity of the gods.

Teacher: Absolutely, and we know that the question of religion is central in the context of ancient Greek philosophy and culture, before the birth of Christianity or Islam. In other words, it is a theme that features prominently in the works of Plato and Aristotle.

Student: Aristotle also states that happiness is an activity that characterizes human beings, rather than animals, which clearly means that there is something rational about the activity which produces happiness?

Teacher: Yes, Aristotle states that happiness is something divine, which is hinted at by the term used for happiness in ancient Greek, 'eudaimonia', from 'daimōn', meaning a spirit or god. This personal god accompanied human beings throughout their lives. Even if happiness is not attained through fortune and is not given to us by the gods, it is something divine in itself, as the activity that characterizes the gods.

Student: Aristotle enquires into the ways in which we attain happiness, which is the ultimate and complete human goal. Happiness is very similar to virtue, is it not?

Teacher: Yes, that is correct, virtue is an end in itself, and so is happiness. They have many things in common. It is not possible to be happy without being virtuous, as we have seen, both for Plato and for Aristotle. For Socrates and for the Stoics, virtue is all one needs in order to be happy. For Aristotle, however, more than virtue is needed, and therefore it may be that happiness is a goal that is even more complete than virtue.

Student: And some external goods might help in the exercise of virtue?

Teacher: We have seen that generosity becomes more easily practiced if one has the means. Aristotle does not accept that virtue comes from fortune, although fortune can contribute to it, and it is unlikely that it is given to us by the gods. It is, like virtue, up to us, at least up to a point. Happiness, like virtue, requires effort on our part; it is like an exercise.

Student: Aristotle also comments on Solon's advice for us to wait until after someone has died in order to pronounce him or her happy?

Teacher: That is right. Because of one's changes in fortune it is only possible to conclude whether someone has been happy after he or she has passed away. In addition, Aristotle considers happiness an activity, and in particular an activity of the soul, and in that sense, happiness must mean something that happens to a living human being. Also, it does not make sense to tie happiness to fortune and honor, for these can change once one has passed away. The way one is perceived can be influenced by the actions of family members, even after one has passed away. Happiness must come primarily as a result of one's deeds, although Aristotle is reluctant to exclude all aspects of fortune and external goods, including one's family, as important contributors to happiness. However, for him happiness has to be something stable and not just momentary joy. The discussion regarding the time when one should be pronounced happy should be understood within that context.

Student: Friendship is an important aspect of virtue, if not a virtue itself, and naturally it requires friends with whom one is friendly? This seems to mean that friends or friendship are external goods?

Teacher: Exactly, friendship is a good example of a good which is not entirely under our control. One may lose one's friends in certain circumstances that are beyond our control. This is why Aristotle does not entirely exclude external goods and fortune from the make-up of happiness. Some external goods are required for the exercise of at least some virtues.

Student: The kind of friendship favored by Aristotle, or the kind that represents the highest form of virtue, seems to develop between two adult males. Some scholars hold that Aristotle's conception of virtue and happiness too is elitist and that it concerns an adult male Greek who is a citizen.

Teacher: There is perhaps some truth in that. Virtue can only be fully attained by adults rather than children, given its association with rationality. Aristotle does not think that animals can be happy either, in the complete sense of happiness. Clearly the fully virtuous and happy person must be free and able to participate in politics, and that clearly means an adult male in ancient Greece, arguably within a democratic context. Socrates, on the other hand, in Plato's dialogue *Meno*, considers the correct definition of virtue to be potentially applicable to all, including women, children and slaves, rather than just adult men. Naturally, for Aristotle, since happiness depends on the practice of virtue and the fulfillment of human nature, which means exercising one's intellect, animals and children cannot be completely included in this picture of those who are able to attain happiness. In the *Politics*, he states that nature, habit, and a rational principle make human beings good and virtuous.

Student: It seems that taking into account local customs can lead to discrimination against certain groups, when one thinks of the attainment of happiness through the complete practice of virtue.

Teacher: Absolutely. This aspect of Aristotle's ethics is likely to have influenced his views on women's and children's capacity for ethical action and the attainment of happiness. The case stands differently with Plato, who has a more abstract or universalist view of virtue.

Student: The question of considering one's happiness ascertainable at the end of one's life is also a very interesting one, as we have seen.

Teacher: Yes, and it is clear that for Aristotle 'eudaimonia' means also blessedness, and a certain closeness to the gods and their typical activity which consists in contemplation. In addition, it becomes clear that for Aristotle happiness does not consist simply in joy or a momentary state, as we have seen, but refers to one's consistent conduct and character as well as external circumstances over the course of one's lifetime. Happiness, then, consists in the practice of virtue, and the possession of certain external goods, over a long period of time.

Student: Catholic theologians will also typically consider blessed those people who have passed away, and after closely examining their life and statements.

Teacher: Absolutely. Blessedness in this case means someone who has led an impeccable life from a religious and ethical perspective. It is a concept, as with sainthood, that indicates the belief that these people will be happy in the next life, even if they have suffered hardship in this life.

Student: It is interesting how virtue, like happiness, appears to depend on us and the decisions we make, but also on external factors, at least for Aristotle and some Aristotelian philosophers. Perhaps there is a certain tension or at least an interplay between these two aspects.

Teacher: This is a very interesting aspect of Aristotle's approach to happiness. For him, happiness is clearly not just dependent on us. For medieval philosophers and theologians, happiness depends primarily on God, and particularly happiness in the next life, which is understood as blessedness. Virtues that are essential for salvation are given to us by God.

Student: You mentioned how Aristotle in the end favors contemplation as the activity that affords most happiness, which means that studying is more rewarding than practicing the moral virtues.

Teacher: Towards the end of the *Nicomachean Ethics*, Aristotle expands on what he means by happiness and how it can be attained. He mentions the advantages of practicing the intellectual over the moral virtues. It seems that perfect happiness comes primarily from the intellectual virtues.

Student: What are the advantages of practicing the intellectual virtues?

Teacher: Aristotle says that one can study in an uninterrupted way, whereas other activities are more difficult to maintain. Interestingly, medieval Islamic philosophers and thinkers, such as Avicenna, also defend the stability of certain activities such as studying, over activities that involve the body. Somehow, the mind differs from the body in the sense of being able to work continuously. If we become tired while studying, that is due to the body, according to these philosophers.

For Aristotle, we do not tire of studying in the same way that we can become tired of engaging in other activities. In addition, studying is a more independent activity than practicing the moral virtue. We can study by ourselves, for instance. Naturally, the philosopher is the person who typically practices this kind of intellectual activity.

Student: It seems that the philosophers are the happiest people.

Teacher: That is right, and in studying and pursuing wisdom they are closer to the gods than other human beings, since the gods also contemplate.

Aquinas, as we will see, thinks of God as virtuous, in the sense of being just and also prudent. However, Aristotle does not think that the gods practice the moral virtues; he thinks of that notion as being beneath the nature and the typical activities of the gods. They do not make contracts, for instance, or control fear and other emotions through courage or temperance, as he states in the *Nicomachean Ethics*.

Student: Those are very different views about the divine nature.

Teacher: Indeed. Self-sufficiency is an important aspect of perfect happiness, according to Aristotle. For the practice of the moral virtues, we may need certain external goods, such as wealth and power, which we do not require in the case of studying. And although happiness is an activity, it is also found in leisure. We return to the dichotomy of the relative merits of the active and the contemplative life.

Student: How does Aristotle conclude his thoughts on that issue?

Teacher: It is curious to see that in the *Nicomachean Ethics*, ethics is a stepping stone to politics, and in that sense, the goal of ethics and of virtue is politics. However, Aristotle states that study is better than engaging in politics and brings greater happiness. While politics serves to help others, there is no ulterior motive for study. Study is a more complete activity in itself, simpler and requiring fewer external factors, and in that sense, study brings complete happiness more than political activity. He also states that understanding is something divine, and that the best life is the one that follows understanding.

Student: And it seems to be difficult to combine both kinds of activities, even today.

Teacher: Perhaps a good example of an ancient philosopher who was also a politician is Cicero.

Student: Yes, he was a famous statesman in Republican Rome, but he also has an extensive philosophical corpus.

Teacher: That is correct, and he was both a successful politician and a serious student of philosophy. However, it appears that he devoted himself to the study and writing of philosophy primarily when, for some reason, he had to abstain from active politics—for instance, if he had to go into exile.

Student: In that case, he would have had little time to devote himself to philosophy while being a politician, and the two activities were not developed at the same time.

Teacher: Perhaps not exactly at the same time. Towards the end of the *Nicomachean Ethics*, Aristotle favors contemplative activity or study over political engagement, even if ethics is a stepping stone to politics.

Student: I understand how, for Aristotle, studying provides a surer path to happiness in the way it is an autonomous activity, depending on ourselves more than on others. It is a more complete or self-contained activity than politics. It also seems to be an activity than is closer to divine action, as Aristotle sees it.

Teacher: That is right, seeing that Aristotle thinks of understanding or intellectual activity as something divine.

Student: At this point, he also seems to prefer the intellectual to the moral virtues.

Teacher: That is a valid impression from reading the conclusion of the *Nicomachean Ethics*. Aristotle often states that the majority of people can hold the wrong opinion, for instance about pleasure or happiness. Moral virtue seems to be more accessible to the majority of people than intellectual virtue. However, the two kinds of virtues are interdependent. Prudence is an important intellectual virtue, but it is closely connected with the moral virtues, in the way that it guides the moral virtues. Aristotle affirms that the excellent or perfectly virtuous person, from a moral point of view, is the model for virtue in general, and we can assume that this includes the intellectual virtues.

Student: Is there another reason why Aristotle may prefer the intellectual virtues?

Teacher: The moral virtues are specifically human, and pertain to our behavior toward others, whereas intellectual virtue points to divine activity. Moreover, he associates moral virtue with emotions and the control of those emotions, which again is something typically human. He also makes a connection between these emotions and the body, which is inferior to the intellect. In the same way, someone engaged in politics also spends more time and effort caring for the body or issues pertaining to the body. In that sense, the intellectual virtues can be regarded as something superior.

At the same time, a certain unity of the virtues is maintained. Aristotle also states that prudence cannot be separated from moral virtue, as we have seen. This one intellectual virtue, prudence, is vital for the practice of the moral virtues.

Student: Aristotle also accepts that anyone can practice the various virtues, does he not?

Teacher: Absolutely, and one does not need to be a politician or a public person in order to practice the virtues.

Notoriety is not important in this sense. One does not need an abundance of external goods in order to be virtuous and practice the virtues, as we have mentioned.

Student: It would seem that the end of the *Nicomachean Ethics* points to both practical and theoretical aspects of Aristotle's works, and not just his politics but also his logical and epistemological works.

Teacher: Yes, and because virtue in any case involves reason, the two aspects cannot be dissociated from each other.

Student: Returning to the question of happiness, I understand how Aristotle, in the *Nicomachean Ethics*, is clearly careful to describe happiness and the way to attain it before going into detail about the nature of virtue and the differences between the various virtues. With regard to happiness, and the need for it to be examined toward the end of one's life, his discussion also raises the question of the kind of happiness we are talking about, whether in this or the next life. It is also patent that he thinks of happiness as hinging on the activity of the soul, especially the intellect, rather than being associated primarily with the body.

Teacher: Yes, and obviously the ancient Greeks also had a conception of happiness in this world and the next. This is very clear in the philosophical literature of that period, such as Plato's *Phaedo*, where Socrates, waiting in prison to be executed, seeks to provide a proof for the immortality of the soul. Towards the end of the dialogue he describes the fate of the souls in the afterlife, and how the good souls will be rewarded while evildoers in this life will be punished. Happiness in this sense means salvation or blessedness in the next life, as we have mentioned. Happiness is then a quality of the soul, particularly in its highest expression, the intellect, rather than the body.

Student: Naturally, other Aristotelian philosophers take up this issue later, and the role of religion is significant?

Teacher: Absolutely. A Catholic theologian like Thomas Aquinas considers happiness in the next life to be complete blessedness, since it cannot then be changed and it is eternal. Happiness in this life is important, but not nearly as important as salvation and blessedness. More generally, and following Aristotle, he describes happiness as an operation according to perfect virtue, and the knowledge of the highest intelligibles, obtained through wisdom. Ultimate happiness or blessedness consists in the use of the intellect.

Student: Then happiness as such, in contrast to blessedness and salvation, is a characteristic of this life?

Teacher: Yes, and it can have some permanence too, in spite of any reverses in fortune.

Student: And Thomas Aquinas also has a different view of the virtues with regard to the next life, does he not?

Teacher: That is correct. While he considers the intellectual and the moral virtues as described by Aristotle, he also develops the theory of the theological virtues, which are three in number, faith, hope and charity, which are specifically aimed at helping us to attain salvation in the next life. These are very important, but since we are focusing on the philosophical rather than the theological aspect of the virtues, we will concentrate on the intellectual and moral virtues.

Student: Aquinas also considers that some of the other virtues come from God, is it not so?

Teacher: According to him the moral virtues can be infused by God. The moral virtues can be naturally acquired or given to us by God. There is natural justice, which is acquired by habituation, and there is infused virtue, which is infused in the soul by God.

Student: How does Aquinas articulate the two kinds of virtues?

Teacher: It is important to understand that the infused virtues specifically prepare human beings for the next life.

Student: It is interesting to think of all the aspects associated with virtue ethics. Is there anything we should discuss further, as a precondition of virtue, or a goal of virtue, before going into a more detailed analysis of the virtues?

Teacher: Yes, perhaps we should discuss further the question of that which is up to us, as Aristotle puts it.

Student: Does that bear on the question of free will and its opposite, determinism?

Teacher: Precisely. It seems that we must presuppose the existence of free will not just within ethics broadly speaking, but also with regard to the more specific question of the virtues.

Student: Could you please be more specific on the ways in which determinism is an obstacle to free will, and how that calls into question the very discipline of ethics?

Teacher: Free will means the ability to choose and it goes hand in hand with rationality, according to the ancient and medieval philosophical tradition. It appears to be something specifically human, according to the philosophers. It then entails bearing responsibility for one's deeds.

Student: Later Aristotelian philosophers, such as Aquinas, and Augustine before him, state that God and the angels have free will.

Teacher: That is right. For Aquinas, wherever there is intellect, there is free will. In the case of the angels, the proof of their free will is the case of the fallen angels, who decided not to obey God. In the case of God, however, God can do no wrong and therefore the case is entirely different. God has free will, since it is something good, but he can never choose to do evil, as that goes against his fundamentally good nature.

Student: How do we prove that we have free will?

Teacher: Perhaps we could have a kind of proof based on human nature, and the way in which we perceive ourselves. There may be another proof, based on the need to defend an ethical perspective, a kind of teleological proof, aiming at the end goal.

We naturally live in society and deal with others. There are different ways of treating other people, justly or unjustly. It is clear that we have a choice as to these different options, and we sense and perceive that we have these options. From our own perspective, as agents, we perceive that freedom of action, which comes from a free will. This free will is really a freedom to choose. We also perceive in us the ability to choose without constraint, or otherwise being forced to take a certain course of action.

Perhaps there is also a proof that human free will exists starting from the end goal, which is the need for ethics. If we are compelled in what we desire and do, human action cannot be considered to be good or bad. Praise or blame are attributed based on our ability to choose, respectively, what is good or bad with regard to a course of action. Ethics discusses the distinction between what is good and what is bad, what is right and wrong in human action, while highlighting and upholding what is good.

Student: This latter approach would consist in proving that we have free will based on our need for ethics, and that free will is a presupposition of ethics?

Teacher: Yes. In a similar way, Kant holds that the proof of God's existence is bound up with morality, in the sense that there is human morality and it presupposes God's existence, since God's existence is the guarantee of morals and the attainment of happiness. God's existence and morality cannot be dissociated, and naturally this is to be understood within the context of Kant's understanding of the limitations of reason, and the need to prove God's existence not through speculative reason and in the domain of metaphysics, but rather through practical reason and in the moral domain.

Student: I understand that free will is the foundation for, and underpins, any ethical theory. Then again, living in society would be impossible without a foundational consideration for ethics and ethical action. The existence of ethics is both real and a necessity for human beings as part of their communal life.

In this sense, I am aware that determinism constitutes an obstacle to ethics and to virtue.

2.3. The Challenge of Determinism

Teacher: There are various kinds of determinism. The main point at stake is that free will means that the decisions we make and the actions we undertake are up to us; in other words, they depend on us and have their starting point in us. This does not mean that every action is a result of free will. There are natural actions which we constantly engage in, such as breathing. However, free will means that we are responsible for and accountable for the actions that matter in terms of human relations, and in the way in which we treat other living beings. We have free will with regard to the actions that are up to us. Only if they are up to us can we be held responsible for them. If we are determined completely or partially by external factors, or by certain internal factors, then we are not responsible and are not to blame, or to be praised.

If our actions are determined, this would mean that we lack the power of decision, and in that case, punishment, human or divine, would have no justification. There would be no ethical action, because human action would come down to some other factor or cause, not a purely human one.

Student: I understand, ethics concerns that which is specifically human, and specifically human agency. In that sense, the subject of ethics would not exist, if human action were due to natural or other external factors. And some important issues debated in ethics, like punishment, and just punishment, as well as the question of justice, would become meaningless, which would call into question the discipline of ethics.

Teacher: As Aristotle states, philosophical disciplines are constituted by a special subject matter, and without free will, as we can see, there would be no specific subject matter of ethics. Human action would be explained by another discipline, such as biology or some other natural science. Ethics studies what is specifically human, and not simply from a natural point of view, which would apply to other animals. Insofar as determinism implies that there is no human free will, it undermines the very discipline of ethics.

Student: As you mentioned, there are different kinds of determinism?

Teacher: Yes, and perhaps some of them can be compatible with the notion of free will. Causal determinism can be understood at the metaphysical or the physical or natural level. It suggests that everything happens due to a cause, and particularly due to a necessary cause. In the case of physical or natural determinism, this is a natural cause. This kind of determinism states that things are the way they are, and that they are necessarily so because of a cause, a necessary cause. If we can think of human agency as independent of external causes, be they natural or external in other ways, then free will is preserved.

Student: In that case, human free will and action would still be independent of external factors, like natural causes?

Teacher: Exactly. A theory defending the combination of determinate natural causes alongside human free will is normally termed compatibilist.

Student: There are also problems if causal determinism is forsaken?

Teacher: Yes, for the natural sciences, like physics, chemistry and biology, it is important that the laws of nature are firmly in place and that they are known to us.

Otherwise, scientific knowledge becomes less reliable. If the laws of nature are stable, we can predict future natural phenomena, but not if the causal chains are not firmly in place or not known.

Naturally, the question of determinism is very complex and we cannot discuss it in detail here. We should explain it in so far as it bears on the question of ethics and specifically free will.

Student: Are there other kind of determinism, in addition to physical or metaphysical determinism?

Teacher: Ethical determinism means that our moral actions are determined, and in that case there is no compatibilism between natural causes and free will. We can also think of psychological determinism as one specific aspect of determinism, if we think that we are determined by our personalities or ways of thinking.

Student: However, if psychological determinism means that those actions are up to us, then perhaps this would not contradict the idea of free will.

Teacher: Free will implies autonomy of the will, which means that the will establishes its own rules and decisions. If we are determined by another part of ourselves, our emotions, for instance, that might take away from our free will and responsibility. Within human nature, free will is part of the will, and should not be determined by some other aspect of ourselves, except reason, which, as we have seen, is closely allied with the will. We will discuss this further when we discuss temperance and the question of the temperate or intemperate person. Sometimes, there is an inner struggle that seems to prevent morally good action. If we follow reason, which is allied with the will, then the action is still up to us. This question naturally depends on the way in which we understand human nature, namely whether reason is the defining aspect of human nature, and whether will and reason are closely connected.

The other problem with psychological determinism is that it would in principle allow psychologists to predict individual human behavior, since the goal of the sciences is also to predict future phenomena based on general laws. If our behavior can be fully predicted, then it is not reconcilable with the notion of free will.

Student: Perhaps an added element can compound this problem, if those traits of character have a biological explanation, in which case we would be talking about biological determinism?

Teacher: Yes, and the same goes for genetic aspects that could perhaps influence our behavior.

Student: Other than nature, can there be other extraneous determinants?

Teacher: Yes, and theological determinism is a very important form of determinism.

Student: It means that God determines our actions.

Teacher: Yes, and it is grounded in the notion of God's power. If God is all-powerful, then He determines all events. This would include natural events and human actions. God would shape human nature and also every single human action.

Student: This is a theological question, and we can discern it in different religions and theological traditions, can we not?

Teacher: That is correct. In Jewish, Christian and Islamic theology this is a very important point, namely how to reconcile God's omnipotence with the notion of human free will and responsibility. There is also the question of God's justice, which can only be in place if human beings are responsible for their actions, since they cannot be justly punished if their actions are not up to them.

Student: Yes, human free will means a kind of power which is specifically the province of human beings. It only becomes a problem in a theological context if we think that attributing this power to humans means to take it away from God, indicating that some crucial events are not caused by God but by human beings?

Teacher: Precisely. Also, in religions in which God is not all-powerful, human free will would in principle not constitute an obstacle to God's power. In Judaism, Christianity and Islam, God is omnipotent, and hence the difficulty in reconciling divine and human agency.

Student: Has this question also preoccupied many theologians and philosophers?

Teacher: Yes, it has been discussed for many centuries if not millennia. Free will is important as a foundation for ethics, as we have seen, but theologians also feel the need to stress God's omnipotence. How to combine the two is a theme that has beset the theologians for a long time. Some theologians stress God's omnipotence without going into details about human free will, while others believe and seek to show that free will is not an obstacle to the affirmation of God's omnipotence. Again, a kind of compatibilism may be sought in this case. We will not go into details on this question, but there are perhaps different kinds of determinism, or ways in which God determines events and substances. He can determine events directly, as stated by those who uphold Islamic occasionalism, or through secondary causes, which would be the position taken by medieval Aristotelian philosophers.

In addition, we can consider this question from the prism of divine attributes, as we have seen. God is omnipotent, but he is also just. In that sense, he cannot justly punish human beings unless they are responsible for their actions, and they can only become responsible if they have power of decision and action.

Student: These are different kinds of theological determinism.

Teacher: That is correct. Some theologians hold that God determines everything directly, a position which has been identified as occasionalism. Other theologians, following the Aristotelian tradition, hold that God determines everything but can delegate his power to secondary causes, as we have seen. Even the term predestination has various meanings. It can broadly mean that God determines the future, and determines everything, or, more specifically, it means that he predestines some people to be saved, in other words, determines in advance that they will be saved, which is the way in which Aquinas, for instance, uses the term 'predestination'. Fate or fatalism is an associated concept and it states that what is bound to happen will happen, without considering the process involved, but simply with a stress on the outcome, which cannot be changed and is beyond our control.

Student: Regardless of the way in which events and substances are caused or determined, involving necessity, there must be a place for free will which is irreducible to necessary conditions outside our control?

Teacher: That is correct. Whether events are substances that are determined as a whole or in part by external factors, whether by nature or God — that is to say, by something external to our will — there must be an element of free will that grounds ethics and ethical action, as well as virtue.

Apart from any theoretical consequences, it is not clear how human societies would function if we did away with the notion of free will, which accounts for what is typically considered human action.

Student: Well, without free will, there would be no responsibility or accountability.

Teacher: Exactly, and punishment, however we conceive it, would also be completely out of place. Whether punishment is seen as a way to redress an evil or to improve the evildoer, it cannot be conceived without attributing responsibility and blame.

Student: There would be no difference between what is done and what ought to be done, and the notion of what ought to be done would be meaningless, and everything would be simply as it is.

Teacher: Yes, the terms contingent and possible would be eliminated from human action.

Student: This would not create an orderly society, but the opposite?

Teacher: Exactly, because there would be no difference between right and wrong, and it would make no sense to impose duties. This would probably lead to chaos in human society. A complete kind of determinism based on the laws of nature, while explaining and accounting for natural events, would lead to a lack of order in human conduct.

Student: It sounds like a kind of paradox, if we try to mix the natural order with the social and human order, or if we subsume the human order under the natural order.

Teacher: Yes, but this shows that there is a kind of human conduct, and rules of conduct that are specific to human society and cannot be inferred from the natural world.

Student: I agree. There has to be a separate kind of causality or norms for human conduct that are not subsumed under natural laws but are separate and autonomous, as stated by Kant as a condition for the existence of free will versus a deterministic outlook.

We have considered the preconditions of virtue, and also of ethics, free will being an essential foundation for any kind of ethics. Are there other specific themes which we may consider as foundational for virtue ethics?

Teacher: More than other kinds of ethical theories, virtue ethics relies on the study and understanding of human nature.

Student: Is there a reason for that specific aspect of virtue ethics?

Teacher: If we think of the three main kinds of ethics or normative ethics that are studied by contemporary scholars, namely virtue ethics, duty ethics, and utilitarianism, we find that in duty ethics the notion of right may be established without a particular regard for human nature, or the source of human action. In fact, this kind of ethics could be established on the basis of human rights and the way one ought to be treated.

Student: Do you have in mind Kant's ethics of duty and his idea of the categorical imperative?

Teacher: That is a good example. When Kant says that each human being should be treated as an end and not as a means, that is a general principle which is founded on the end goal of ethics. Human beings should not be handled as a means to an end but as the end itself. There are also other rules that are absolute and do not change according to circumstances and that apply to all individuals, such as the principle which enjoins us not to lie.

Student: Perhaps that kind of ethics, like Kantian ethics, can be viewed as having developed from the top down, whereas virtue ethics, at least in Aristotle's case, appears to be built from the bottom up, with a firm basis on his understanding of human nature and what is suitable to it.

Teacher: Yes, although there could be some variations and combinations of those two alternatives. Naturally, Kant's ethics appears to be based on a legal model, where the rules are established and then applied universally, regardless of individual persons or circumstances. In Aristotle's case, virtue is a development of human nature and consists in the development of a disposition that then becomes a habit and a firmly established character trait.

Student: In the case of Plato, virtue appears to be drawn from his theory of forms, in the sense that the virtues are forms as universal concepts.

Teacher: That is right, and in that case, knowledge of the universal concept or the form would be the key to knowing and practicing each virtue. However, Kant's ethics is believed to have been influenced by important developments in the field, in particular the notion of a law-giving deity who imposes the laws from above.

Student: Naturally, that is a development derived from a monotheistic religion such as Christianity?

Teacher: Yes, that is naturally a very important, indeed a decisive influence.

Student: Can we find a combination of the two models?

Teacher: Yes, we can find that combination in Aquinas, where the two traditions, the Aristotelian one and the Biblical one, are found side by side. Aquinas harmonizes them, even if one can debate the details of that combination of traditions.

Student: Perhaps his understanding of the different types of virtues is proof of that harmonization?

Teacher: Indeed, we have seen how the infused virtues come from God while the natural moral virtues come from us. There is also a close connection between the good, human nature and the way in which God establishes the natural law.

Student: Does Aquinas make place for individual differences in his understanding of virtue?

Teacher: Yes, in the case of the Aristotelian tradition, virtue is about the mean, as we will see, but that mean can vary from person to person.

Student: Could we also say that virtue ethics is more particularistic in that sense?

Teacher: That is true in the case of Aristotle, and even Aquinas, but not in the case of Plato, who advocates for a more universalistic conception of virtue.

Student: Could we say that Kant's ethics is aligned with a notion of human nature which is based on human reason, in other words, human nature as identified with reason?

Teacher: I think it is fair to say that Kant privileges the rational aspect of human beings, and thus he views human nature as essentially rational.

Student: In what sense, then, is Aristotelian virtue ethics based on human nature?

Teacher: It is clear that for Aristotle, ethics is not a rigorous science. This means that it is not based on universal principles, or a universal science. He develops his theory of ethics on the basis of his understanding of human nature in its diversity.

Student: He differs from Plato in that respect?

Teacher: Yes. Plato thinks of virtue as a form, and of the good as a form, as we have seen. And the forms are universal principles, and apply to all instances which bear the name of the form. For Aristotle, virtue is also at the center of ethics, but he thinks that it can vary from person to person and from region to region. Also, as we will see, the virtues are not acquired simply through knowledge, but also through habituation and practicing virtuous acts. There is something very practical about virtue, for Aristotle, like a craft that is developed.

Student: But unlike a craft, it does not produce an object but a virtuous action?

Teacher: Exactly. And there are also differences between the moral virtues and the intellectual virtues. The latter are acquired through learning, but the former are acquired through habituation, which seems to point to a method of trial and error.

Student: In what sense, then, is virtue ethics reliant on the idea of human nature?

Teacher: This connection between virtue and human nature is particularly clear in Aristotle. Virtue is developed by habituation and it must follow a certain process. Children are not expected to be virtuous, except after a while and after practicing good deeds. Therefore, Aristotle's virtue ethics takes into account particular aspects of human development as one grows up.

Student: Can we say that, for Aristotle, virtue is something natural?

Teacher: Aristotle thinks of virtue as something natural, pertaining to human beings, and constituting the fulfillment of human nature. However, natural in this context does not mean that virtue is an inborn capacity. Rather, it has to be developed. We are born with a predisposition for virtue, but it has to be developed and it requires a sustained effort. In addition, as we have seen, virtue requires the use of reason, which is a specifically human characteristic.

Student: And in other kinds of ethics, the natural aspect is not as obvious?

Teacher: In utilitarianism, there does not seem to be a great concern for the agent, and the outcome of the action is what matters, even if the result will ultimately benefit humanity. The means is not as important as the end.

Student: While for Kant, would ethics not be natural to humans?

Teacher: It would only be natural if we were purely rational beings, but there is more to human beings than just rationality. For Kant, ethical action should be based on universal principles, and as such it does not take account of individual human nature, or of feelings and emotions. I do not think that Kant holds us to be purely rational beings, and for him ethical action depends fundamentally on following universal principles without personal satisfaction or feeling in performing an action.

3. Human Nature

3.1. Pleasure, Community and the Emotions

Student: Are there other ways in which virtue theory can be developed based on a certain conception of human nature?

Teacher: For Aristotle, virtue is natural since we are naturally predisposed to it, although it must be acquired through effort. For him, virtue takes account of different personalities and circumstances. And for him, the virtuous person does virtuous deeds with pleasure, which again is a sign of an alignment with human nature. Pleasure in acting virtuously means that virtue becomes natural to us, once we become used to acting virtuously. More broadly, he thinks of human beings as rational animals, and the two aspects, rationality and aspects related to the fact that we belong to the animal genus, must be taken into account in developing an ethical theory.

Student: I understand the significance of pleasure in this context. We looked into the connection between pleasure and happiness, but the link between pleasure and human nature is also important.

Teacher: It is an essential point for Aristotle. Virtue is something that develops based on human nature, and pleasure in doing virtuous action means that one has become adept at acting virtuously, and that the virtues have been truly acquired. In his *Commentary on the* Nicomachean Ethics, Aquinas also stresses this point, namely, the link between pleasure and virtue. Indeed, Aristotle associates virtue and vice respectively with pleasure and pain.

Student: There must be good and bad pleasures, too.

Teacher: Yes, and for Aristotle, pleasure is an activity and an end, rather than a becoming, although this is a complex matter. We have discussed the link between good and pleasure, but it is important to analyze the link between pleasure and virtue.

Student: We have mentioned a distinction between bodily or physical pleasure and intellectual pleasure.

Teacher: That is right, and Aristotle thinks of pleasure as something good. True pleasure is something that respects nature, such as the restoration of health, and it is something that is within the right measure. For instance, if we drink the right amount of liquids and eat the right amount of food, that is pleasurable, but eating too much or too little causes pain. However, pain is not always opposed to pleasure in every case. Aristotle also holds that there can be pleasure without pain or appetite, as in the case of the pleasure we take in studying. This kind of pleasure makes us want to study more. In virtue there is a mean, and there can be a mean in pleasure. In the case of the intellectual virtues and intellectual pleasures, the higher extreme seems better than an exact mean. However, Aquinas, who also defends the doctrine of the mean in the case of the virtues, states that the mean in the case of the intellectual virtues is the truth, constituting the right amount and the right target, as he states in the *Summa Theologiae*.

Student: Is there a pleasure typical of the virtuous person?

Teacher: The temperate person, who controls the passions and bodily pleasures, avoids excesses that will not lead to true pleasure. However, the pleasures that involve excesses are the bodily pleasures, so Aristotle seems to hint at the possibility that the temperate person does not focus on physical pleasure, which can lead to excesses, but tends to seek the intellectual pleasures. Pleasures that do not involve pain do not have an excess, and those tend to be intellectual rather than physical pleasures. The pleasant also accords with our nature. In that sense, it is assumed that rational activity is what is proper to adult human beings, and therefore intellectual or rational pleasure is the most laudable one in that it allows us to develop and complete our nature.

Student: Aristotle emphasizes the notion of pleasure as activity, does he not?

Teacher: That is correct. Perhaps one can be active without exerting oneself or without undergoing change. For

Aristotle, the gods are the paradigm of perfect activity and pleasure, but change signifies a lack of perfection, and therefore this must be an activity which does not imply change. He argues that there is more pleasure in rest than in change.

Student: Is there a Platonic influence in defending the association of perfection with changelessness?

Teacher: Perhaps there is, since the forms are the paradigms of perfection for Plato, and they are changeless but also active.

Student: Returning to the question of pleasure, can we say that there are good and bad pleasures?

Teacher: Aristotle makes a distinction between pleasure and the good, and he also holds that not every pleasure is choice-worthy. However, he thinks of pleasure as something complete. We have seen that some pleasures are better than others because they do not admit of excess, such as the pleasure of studying. It seems that the best pleasures are those that are of an intellectual nature. When it comes to physical pleasures, there has to be a right measure.

Student: Perhaps there is a certain parallelism in this sense between virtue and pleasure, since both consist in a mean.

Teacher: That is the case for some, but not all, kinds of pleasure. Bodily pleasures consist in a mean, like eating the right amount, while studying does not seem to consist in a mean, just like the pleasure which results from practicing the intellectual virtues.

Student: Aristotle also explores the connection between pleasure and activity.

Teacher: That is correct. We have seen that pleasure consists in a kind of activity, and this pertains also to the use of the senses. We delight in seeing and hearing certain things.

Student: Does it mean to take pleasure simply in perceiving?

Teacher: Aristotle states that this consists in perceiving the object in the right condition. One might add that it depends on what we see and hear, and not simply on hearing and seeing. In that sense, pleasure has to do with the object perceived or contemplated, and not just with the activity. As such, pleasure results from the activity.

Student: Does this mean continuous activity?

Teacher: We may become tired of constant activity, when we use the senses. Aristotle states that we delight in perceiving new things, and then can become tired of them.

Student: Is there also a comparison between physical and intellectual perception?

Teacher: Perhaps, and this a point developed later, for instance, by medieval Islamic philosophers, such as Avicenna. He stated that the senses become weaker with age, but not the intellect. And if the intellect becomes tired, it is because of the tiredness of the body. The intellect itself does not tire of studying.

Student: This entails a focus on the spiritual side of human beings as opposed to the physical aspect.

Teacher: I agree, and perhaps a parallelism with the case of pleasure can be found. Intellectual pleasure does not tire us, but we can become tired of physical pleasures, which in any case should observe the right measure. Aristotle also states that each animal has its own kind of pleasure, which indicates that human pleasure should be intellectual, in accordance with human nature.

Student: Aristotle also draws a comparison between life and pleasure.

Teacher: Pleasure derives from being a living being, and pleasure is a sign of being alive, which is also an activity. Pleasure comes from life and the activities that are proper to each of us, and Aristotle states that pleasure also completes life, as a more perfect activity. Pleasure presupposes and completes an activity, or it results from the completion of an activity.

Student: Does pleasure pertain to the end more than the beginning of the activity?

Teacher: According to Aristotle in the *Nicomachean Ethics*, pleasure is grounded in an activity and it leads to the increase of that activity. He gives the example of geometry and the fact that we become better geometers if we love geometry. In that way, it seems that pleasure is a motive force as well as an aid in completing an activity, in the sense that it leads to a particular activity and it results from it.

Student: For Aristotle, pleasure is something multifaceted?

Teacher: Yes, it can be physical or intellectual. Plato had also debated the question of pleasure in the *Philebus*, where we find a distinction between physical and intellectual pleasures. For Aristotle, each activity affords its proper pleasure, like flute playing. I suppose this also means that different people can take pleasure in different activities. However, at the same time, there seems to be some objective measure of pleasure, in the sense that some physical pleasures are perhaps not appropriate. In addition, as in the case of virtue, the measure of true pleasure is the virtuous or excellent person. Good pleasures are those in which the good person delights. In fact, the good person is the measure of each thing.

Student: Does Aquinas have a different view on pleasure?

Teacher: Aquinas does not deny the significance of pleasure as something natural, and something that can lead to an increase in good activities. However, in commenting on Aristotle's views on pleasure, Aquinas accepts celibacy, for instance, as something valid and not as something that indicates insensitivity, because celibate people still enjoy other pleasures.

Student: This seems to be a very different position from that of the Stoics, for instance.

Teacher: A Stoic position would devalue pleasure, given perhaps its irrational nature or its association with the passions. However, delighting in that which is good always seems to be a good thing.

Student: Kant in turn holds that pleasure is at odds with ethical action?

Teacher: For Kant ethical action is independent of particular or emotional aspects.

Student: This means that a natural approach to virtue is particularly prominent in Aristotle. Does that mean that virtue ethics must be based on this kind of naturalism?

Teacher: Yes, we could think of it in that way, especially if we have in mind Aristotle's virtue ethics. For philosophers who strongly emphasize the rational aspect in human beings, to the neglect of other aspects, virtue is attainable by human beings by means of rational activity. In other words, it is possible to defend a kind of virtue ethics which is not naturalistic. In that sense, virtue is something that we should strive to attain, but not as a continuation of our nature as a whole. Aristotle's virtue ethics presupposes a possibly more rounded view of human nature, as including also emotions, and the role of the body.

Student: When it comes to the question of human nature, there is also the issue of whether human nature is good or bad. This is a very broad question, but perhaps it would be good to discuss it before analyzing the nature of virtue in more detail?

Teacher: This is a complex question, and more recently there have been attempts to address it, not only in the philosophical literature. Philosophers like Aristotle and Cicero think of human nature as fundamentally good. This is clear from their assumption that human beings tend to associate and live together, and not just for the sake of the ready supply of material needs. In addition, there are different types of community. Among interpersonal relationships, we can distinguish between a community of two people, or a small group of people, for instance, and larger communities. The political community, the political state, is the largest kind of human community.

Student: Living within a larger community is different from living in a family, then?

Teacher: Precisely. The kind of community in question depends on the number of its members and also the type of relationships between them, as well as the relations of power to be found in those communities. In a family, the parents tend to have the authority, but in a larger community without specific blood ties, it is a different matter. However, several philosophers view the smaller associations, like the family, as building blocks for the larger political association. At any rate, these associations are natural and we naturally seek the company of other people, according to many philosophers.

Student: Is the need for association indicative of the natural goodness of human beings?

Teacher: That depends on the way the association formed. If it is formed naturally, in the sense that it does not require an explicit agreement, even if it does not exclude such agreement later, it can be seen as indicating the goodness of human nature.

Student: Philosophers imagine the first human communities as having formed in different ways?

Teacher: Exactly. For instance, Cicero presupposes that the first communities were formed in a natural way, rather than by any kind of imposition, internal or external. Those who think in this way hold that human beings naturally live together and naturally enjoy being in each other's company, as well as wishing to help others, without further aims, even if the community is also necessary for the supply of basic needs.

Student: However, other philosophers do not believe that this kind of community is natural?

Teacher: That is right. In the modern period, several philosophers defend the principle of the social contract, which means that this kind of community is not natural, since it is not constituted without a specific decision to unite and the reflection on specific rules to be adopted, but is a conscious act to live together.

Student: Is there a particular reason for a change in approach to the way in which political communities are formed?

Teacher: Naturally, if a community is born based on a conscious decision, then the rules guiding that community must be agreed on from the start, and they can also be called into question and changed. In particular, the relationship between the ruler and the ruled can be changed and reformulated. In addition, the social contract theory presupposes that there was a state of nature previous to the social contract, and the way in which philosophers think about that state of nature also tells us what they essentially thought about human nature. In the state of nature, there are no established laws, and human beings live alone or in some kind of community without strictly agreed upon laws and rules.

Student: We have seen that philosophers who view the political community as forming in a natural and seamless way tend to think of human nature as naturally good, in the sense that human beings wish to live with one another and to cooperate.

Teacher: That is right, and once the community is formed, there are different degrees of naturalness. Plato believes in a quite rigid structure with different classes that have different tasks, according to their mental and physical abilities, while Aristotle describes different kinds of political systems with different constitutions. We also know that democracy was born in Athens, in the 5th century BC, and that it is a different system from the one which Plato, for instance, advocates as the best political system.

Student: And among the philosophers who defend the theory of the social contract, do they believe in the goodness of human nature?

Teacher: Rousseau, for instance, believes that human beings are naturally good and they are only corrupted by society and civilization, although he admits that it is currently not possible to live in isolation and return to the state of nature. Someone like Hobbes, writing before Rousseau, believes that the political community and the social contract serve to curb people's naturally violent nature, which means that in the state of nature, before the social contract is established, human beings are violent and naturally attack each other.

Student: In that case, as we have mentioned, the way in which philosophers describe the state of nature is the way in which they view human nature?

Teacher: Yes, because in the state of nature human beings are not limited by laws, only by the natural law. Rousseau believes that human beings are good in the state of nature, as he describes it in the *Discourse on the Origin of Inequality*. However, it is not clear how they are virtuous, since according to Rousseau, in the state of nature human beings live alone—that is to say, there are no human communities and each human being lives in isolation, only occasionally encountering other human beings.

Student: Does Rousseau mention virtue, then, and in what sense?

Teacher: It appears to me that, according to Rousseau, in the state of nature human beings are good in the sense that they do not harm other human beings or other animals. In the state of nature, human beings do not compete with each other. Their natural goodness is indicated by their peaceful state and empathy with other sentient beings, which means that they refrain from harming other humans or other sentient beings. This harmony with the rest of nature is also due to empathy or pity, which means that they treat others in a humane way. For Rousseau, natural morality is founded on the principle of empathy. It is only when human beings have to live together that they start competing and forget their natural empathy or pity, which loses its strength when human beings start living in communities.

Student: However, Hobbes views the state of nature differently?

Teacher: Yes, Rousseau is very critical of Hobbes because for Hobbes the state of nature is a state of war, whereas for Rousseau the warlike conditions only begin when people start living together.

Student: Then Rousseau considers human beings to be good and truly moral in the state of nature?

Teacher: That is correct; his conception of human nature as good is fundamentally linked to the state of nature.

Student: It seems that many philosophers believe in the goodness of human nature, with some exceptions?

Teacher: In the ancient, medieval, and modern traditions, it appears that most philosophers hold that human beings are good, with some exceptions, like that of Hobbes. Shaftesbury thinks of being good to others and living in community as the natural tendency in us, while seeking solitude is unnatural and a sign of an unhappy character.

Student: What would be a clear sign that a philosopher thinks of human nature as good?

Teacher: There could be several signs. For instance, Aristotle holds that virtue is natural, even if it is not exactly an inborn quality, since it has to be developed through practice and habit. This means that there is potential for virtue and good deeds, which is the natural inclination of human beings, under the right circumstances. The fact that virtue is conceived as the perfection of human nature also means that human nature is fundamentally expected to be virtuous, from start to finish, and it seems that virtue is the natural destiny of human beings. In addition, it is not possible to be happy without being virtuous, and this position is also very clear in Plato's works.

Student: What about other philosophers?

Teacher: It should be possible to infer each philosopher's views on human nature by reading what they say about ethics, and several positions can be found on this issue. However, if philosophers insist on the possibility of ethical action, then human beings naturally have an aptitude to perform good deeds.

Student: However, perhaps ethics is that which corrects human nature and ensures that human beings are ready to work towards the common good, and help others, instead of acting in a selfish way?

Teacher: That is also a good justification for the existence of ethics as a practical discipline, with the aim of curbing people's selfish instincts. That would be the position of Hobbes, who proposes sanctions, and some contemporary philosophers.

Student: Then ethical action could be seen as naturally issuing from human nature, if the latter is good, or required in order to correct human nature, if it is seen as bad or essentially selfish.

Teacher: That is right, but in fact many authors discern both altruistic and selfish aspects in human nature, and that is perhaps the most balanced position.

Student: That kind of balance which should be observed is also present in the various virtues?

Teacher: Yes, in seeking to practice the virtues the middle term should be observed and excesses on both ends should be avoided. And, as we have mentioned, some virtues specifically regard our treatment of others, like justice, whereas others are more self-regarding, like temperance, which serves to curb excesses in each of us, when it comes to eating, for instance.

Student: However, it seems that many philosophers count on the goodness of human nature. Would there be a good argument for that position?

Teacher: Perhaps an argument for the goodness of human nature could be built on the general goodness to be found in the world. Medieval philosophers, especially those who follow the Neoplatonic tradition, think of the good as prevailing over evil, for instance Avicenna. They argue for the concept of the order of the good, which indicates God's providence in the way he manages the world. Al-Ghazali, a medieval Muslim theologian, argues that this is the best of all possible worlds, a position later echoed by Leibniz. The implication in this view is that if evil prevailed in the world, the world would have already been destroyed. The same can be said for human communities.

Evil exists, in this case moral evil, and even if it seems to be something real (Plotinus considered evil to be a privation of the good, rather than something substantial or independently real), societies would not function if evil prevailed. It also seems difficult to see how the laws could dissuade people if human beings were essentially selfish. Naturally we possess both selfish and altruistic motives, but there have to be essentially good motives in order for human societies to be able to function. The laws are there to prevent a minority of those who intend to do evil from harming the majority who are well intentioned.

For Christian philosophers, the doctrine of original sin has important consequences for their views on human nature, since it assumes a tendency to do evil within human beings. However, one could still view human nature as initially good, at least before the occasion of original sin, namely the Fall of Adam and Eve. In addition, there are means to attenuate the consequences of original sin, which render possible virtuous action. Christians hold that the sacrament of baptism removes the effects of original sin and restores original human nature.

Student: Is it possible to study the question of human nature from a scientific point of view?

Teacher: The question of virtue, and whether people are virtuous, is so broad that, it seems to me, scientific experimentation cannot provide conclusive proof through repeated single experiments.

Student: Some contemporary philosophers think of virtue as having a corrective nature.

Teacher: Yes, and perhaps we should think of how that affects our conception of human nature. For Aristotle, virtue needs to be practiced and it is something hard to obtain. At the same time, it issues from human nature and perfects it. There may be corrective aspects to virtue, but for Aristotle and Aquinas, for instance, virtue is firmly grounded in human nature. It is not something imposed from outside, as an external rule.

Student: Returning to the question of the emotions, we have seen how Plato, Aristotle, and the Stoics approach the role of the emotions. How does Aquinas, as an Aristotelian philosopher, view the emotions? The emotions or passions are also very important for him, and we should discuss them in order to understand his approach to virtue.

Teacher: That is correct. The term 'passion' is literally associated with undergoing action, and with being passive. For Aquinas, it means to receive and to have something taken.

Student: Are there negative connotations?

Teacher: For Aquinas, if change is for the worse, it more appropriately receives the name of passion than affection. In addition, the passions are aligned with the appetitive part of the soul, rather than the apprehensive part. They are also associated with potentiality and with defect, in the sense of something that is missing.

Student: Aquinas states that the sensitive appetite divides into the irascible and the concupiscible.

Teacher: That is right, and some passions go hand in hand with the irascible power, while others belong to the concupiscible power.

Student: Which ones are found in the irascible power, and which are found in the concupiscible power?

Teacher: The goods that are hard to obtain are the object of the irascible faculty, and goods in general are the object of the concupiscible faculty. Concupiscence is a cognate of desire in a broad sense. However, even the irascible passions revert to the concupiscible passions.

Student: Why is that the case?

Teacher: Because love or desire is the basis of all the passions, as stated by Augustine. We are attracted to that which is good and repelled by that which is evil.

Student: Are there particular emotions or passions associated with each of these two faculties?

Teacher: The concupiscible faculty includes love and hatred, desire and aversion, joy and sadness, while the irascible passion includes hope and despair (both regarding a good which has not yet been obtained), fear (with regard to an evil which is not yet present) daring and anger (arising from a present evil). These are the eleven passions described by Aquinas in the *Summa Theologiae*. By themselves, the passions are not good or evil, but if considered in connection with reason, and in particular with will which is rational appetite, they can become good, or evil if right reason is not followed.

Student: One might say that the passions or emotions cannot be good or evil, if they are involuntary. We cannot be blamed or held responsible for the emotions and for the way in which we feel about things, if we cannot control our emotions. Obviously, that would imply a clear separation between reason and the emotions, the latter being more akin to instincts that we cannot control, like bodily functions.

Teacher: There are different questions that come to mind when we think about the emotions; in addition, different philosophers have viewed them in different ways. We can consider the emotions as being more or less aligned with reason and with the will, and this also depends on how we conceive the will. As we have seen, for Aquinas the will is rational appetite. With regard to the passions, he states that the movements of our limbs are good or evil if they are considered voluntary, and the sensitive appetite, which includes the irascible and concupiscible passions, is closer to reason than are the limbs or outward members. Therefore, these passions are even more likely to be subject to reason and the will, and therefore we cannot say that they are irrational and uncontrollable.

Aquinas also states that justice and the other virtues should be accompanied by a passion, presumably because this is an intrinsic aspect of human nature, and also because moral virtue does not annul the sensitive appetite, but makes it obey reason. Even if virtues are practiced without reference to passion, such as justice — a virtue which is about operations rather than controlling the passions (which is the purpose of temperance and fortitude) — some passion should result from practicing a virtue, for instance, joy. For Aquinas, the more perfect the virtue, the more passion it produces, as an overflow from reason to the sensitive appetite.

The related question of knowledge is also important, and contemporary philosophers and psychologists find a connection between the intellect and the emotions. They argue that the emotions have a cognitive aspect in the sense that they imply a certain belief, and they are based on beliefs. For instance, we may be afraid of things we do not know because we think that they are dangerous or can be dangerous.

Student: Is it possible that passions are not controlled by reason or the will?

Teacher: Aquinas states that the passions are voluntary if they are commanded by the will or if they are not checked by the will.

Student: Is there perhaps a side of the will which is not entirely rational? If animals have a will, but not free will, then the will is not completely rational, since animals are not rational, according to Aquinas.

Teacher: The will implies movement towards some good, and in that sense, animals also seek what is good for them. However, they do not have free will because this implies a dependence on reason, a choice based on knowledge. Perhaps the will is sometimes more about appetite and desire than about rationality, in the case of animals. But in human beings, will is rational appetite. This is obviously a rationalistic reading of the will. In us, the will cannot be truly independent of reason.

Student: Could there be cases where the will or the passions are independent of reason in us?

Teacher: That is a problem that has preoccupied philosophers since at least Plato. Aristotle considers this question, and also Aquinas, and it is illustrated in the examples of intemperance and incontinence, which happen when the appetites overcome reason, and one is tempted and follows these appetites against the judgment of reason. We will discuss this question later in connection with the opposite of virtue, namely, vice.

Student: Does Aquinas compare his views on the emotions with other positions?

Teacher: Yes, in the *Summa Theologiae* he studies the emotions before proceeding to habit and virtue. He also explains different approaches to the emotions by different philosophers. He notes that according to the Stoics, all passions are evil, in opposition to the Aristotelian or Peripatetic philosophers, who favored moderate passions. He explains that the Stoics did not distinguish between sense and intellect, or intellective and sensitive appetite, presumably for the purpose of knowledge, and therefore they did not distinguish between different types of appetite. Consequently, for them there was no difference between the passions of the soul and the movements of the will, whereas for Aquinas the former ones belong to the sensitive appetite and the latter belong to the intellectual appetite. The distinction they make, according to Aquinas, is between the will as a rational movement of the appetite, and the passions which go beyond the limits of reason.

Student: Does that mean that they saw no connection between the passions and reason, and did not integrate the passions with the intellectual nature of human beings?

Teacher: That would be a good way of summing up Aquinas' position on the Stoic theory of the passions. He adds that according to Cicero, in the *Tusculan Disputations*, the Stoics hold the passions to be nothing more than diseases of the soul—and therefore something to be avoided or eliminated. However, in the *Summa Theologiae* he quotes Augustine to the effect that the Stoics accept three passions, namely desire or will, joy and caution, which are good passions and do not stand in the way of reason.

Student: Nevertheless Aquinas holds that the Peripatetic philosophers have a different position on the passions?

Teacher: Yes, according to Aquinas, the Aristotelian philosophers view the passions in a broader way as describing any movement in the sensitive appetite, and therefore regard them as good if they are controlled by reason. Aquinas himself thinks that Cicero should have followed the Peripatetics in seeing a mean in the passions, and as something good. Instead, Aquinas holds that Cicero follows the Stoics in viewing the passions as diseases of the soul, in the same way that the body can be diseased. For Aquinas, that is only the case with the passions if they are not controlled by reason. If they are controlled by reason, they go along with virtue. Reason directs the passions of the sensitive appetite and the operations of the will.

Student: In that case, for the Stoics the presence of the passions in an action is detrimental to the goodness of the action?

Teacher: Exactly, that is what Aquinas says.

Student: That reminds one of Kant's view on the passions as having no positive role in the context of ethical action. Does Aquinas give a reason for the importance of the presence of the passions when it comes to ethical or moral action?

Teacher: He states that the passions are an integral part of human beings, and if they come under the control of reason, then reason is extended and becomes more powerful. The passions are a powerful motor and a force for the good, but only if they are controlled by reason, not if they precede and dominate reason. If the passions follow in the footsteps of reason, they can show the strength of the will, and increase the goodness of the action.

Student: How does reason control the passions?

Teacher: Reason does not let itself be dominated by the passions, but it can let itself be affected by them in a positive and effective way.

Student: Is there an order between the concupiscible and the irascible passions?

Teacher: Since love is the most basic passion and the first of the concupiscible passions, all passions of the irascible faculty also revert to the concupiscible passions. Aquinas adds that the concupiscible passions are more complex than the irascible passions, because the latter imply only movement, since they concern the attainment of something hard to obtain, while the former contain movement and rest.

Student: How is movement and rest implied in the concupiscible passions?

Teacher: Like for Aristotle, the end goal of the will is the good, and for Aquinas the good has the aspect of an end. We seek the end and then rest in the end, delighting in it, resulting in joy. The general aptitude for the good is called love, the desire for it represents the movement, which is concupiscence proper, and joy consists in resting in the good or the end. The process goes from love to joy through desire. Like Cicero, Aquinas lists four main passions, joy and sadness (concerning a present good or evil, respectively) and hope and fear (concerning a future good or evil, respectively). All passions culminate in these four.

Student: If love is such an important passion, as the basis for all passions, does it also exist in non-rational animals?

Teacher: Yes, it exists in them as natural appetite, which we also possess, and by which natural beings seek that which suits their nature. This is based on an apprehension, and therefore it has a cognitive aspect, but interestingly Aquinas states that that kind of apprehension comes from God, and not from the subject of that specific appetite. In addition, there is an appetite which happens in the subject of the appetite and arises from necessity, and this constitutes sensitive appetite. In us, that kind of appetite can follow reason. In addition to those two kinds of appetite, we possess the rational appetite, which is based on an apprehension which is in us, and follows freely from that apprehension.

Student: I understand that there are three types of appetite, corresponding to the vegetative, the sensitive and the rational soul. We have discussed the way in which sensitive appetite can be controlled by reason in us. Does this concern the broad theme of the control of the passions?

Teacher: Yes, and we have seen that the passions involve movement, and that the sensitive or animal part of the soul is also responsible for movement. Even if we do not think of the passions in accordance with the Aristotelian conception of the soul, the term 'passion' or 'emotion' clearly indicates the notion of being moved, and thus indicates movement.

Student: We know that we can control emotions like anger, and that there is a cognitive basis to those emotions. Is it possible for reason to control the natural appetite?

Teacher: In principle, no, if we think of nutrition or digestion, for instance, as part of the natural appetite. However, although the natural appetite controls the feeling of hunger, we can still decide when to eat. Clearly reason has a dominant function in the human soul.

Student: If love is the fundamental passion, for Aquinas as for Augustine, in what ways is it expressed or said?

Teacher: Aquinas refers to love, dilection, charity and friendship. He thinks of love as being more general. In that sense, friendship is a kind of love. Love and dilection are more like an act or a passion, or expressed as such, whereas friendship is a habit. Dilection implies a choice in addition to love, and as such it is purely rational. Charity consists in a perfection of love.

Student: In Latin 'charity' means love, rather than charity in the more specific sense of an offer of financial help?

Teacher: Exactly. And of these four terms, friendship can be considered to be a virtue or like a virtue, since it is a habit, something that is practiced habitually, and not just a passion. Charity is a very important theological virtue, but it takes its name from a passion, like the other two theological virtues, namely hope and faith.

Student: Aquinas also seems to believe in different types and degrees of love.

Teacher: Yes. He also examines benevolence, which consists in wishing others well, as a kind of love, following Aristotle.

Student: The question of the emotions or affections is also central for Shaftesbury, is it not? If we think of the association between virtue and emotion as an essential alliance, then Shaftesbury is one of the modern British philosophers who instantly comes to mind.

Teacher: Yes, this is very important for him within the context of the debate concerning virtue. In his *Inquiry Concerning Virtue and Merit*, which is part of his work *Characteristics of Men, Manners, Opinions*, benevolence is the source of the virtues. For him, there is a strong connection between benevolence, the world order as a sign of God's providence, and beauty. There is an order of the universe to which we are attuned. Naturally, we also possess selfish interests that concern us, in addition to altruistic feelings and motivations. However, ethics is based on the notion of benevolence.

Student: Is there an epistemological basis to this theory?

Teacher: Shaftesbury's thought was very influential and he became associated with the movement of the British moralists, who emphasize the emotions over reason. A philosopher like Hume does not accept an essential connection between reason and moral behavior, but rather bases moral behavior on feeling, in particular sympathy, and views the virtues from the prism of feelings. He went on to become more famous than Shaftesbury, due to his influence on Kant, among other factors, but Shaftesbury is arguably a foundational figure in modern ethics.

As for the epistemological aspect, it is central for him, because our moral sense is not just the result of the affections, and in particular benevolence; rather it is based on our ideas about the world and, even more so, about God. In the *Inquiry Concerning Virtue or Merit*, one's views on God are very important for the way in which one behaves. It is the religious question which prompts the fundamental debates within this *Inquiry*.

Student: How does the idea of God influence our morals, according to Shaftesbury?

Teacher: For Shaftesbury, God is like a role model for human behavior. The question asked in this essay addresses the connection between morals and religion, and that is how it is framed, namely whether being virtuous requires being religious and the practice of religion, or whether morality is independent of religion and religious practice.

Therefore, the question of religion and our conception of God is always in the background. In addition, the question of the origin of the world and how it is ruled is also important, because we tend to attribute a cause to that order and that cause is God. But different people view the world and the worldly order in different ways, and this also affects their conception of the cause of that order.

Student: What types of positions does Shaftesbury discern regarding the cause of the world?

Teacher: He lists four types of positions, the theists, the atheists, the polytheists and the daemonists. Theists believe that everything is ruled for the best by a benevolent principle and mind, while atheists believe that everything happens according to chance and not for a purpose. A polytheist believes that there are several deities governing the world, for the good. Daemonists believe that there are several ruling principles which are not necessarily good.

Student: Does he identify these beliefs with particular groups of people?

Teacher: Shaftesbury does not seem to have particular groups of people in mind, or particular times in history. In fact, he states that people are not consistent in their beliefs and can hold different positions about God at different times, and there are even combinations of these positions. However, theism is clearly the belief in just one God, and it can be identified with Christianity, and perhaps other religions. In turn, atheists do not believe in a guiding benevolent principle of the universe, and polytheists can perhaps be identified with the prevalent beliefs in ancient Greece and Rome. At one point, Shaftesbury gives the example of Jupiter as an example that should not be followed. All these views involve religion except atheism. Some ancient philosophers held that the world came to be by chance and therefore this position is perhaps present at any time in history, and it could be identified with a typical atheistic position.

Student: In ancient Greece and Rome many believed in the goddess of fortune. It seems like believing in a principle that manages a disordered universe.

Teacher: Yes, and perhaps parallels can be found in other world religions. Ancient Greek and Roman religion did not survive, but some older polytheistic religions are still alive today, and there may be equivalent deities. However, I believe that what Shaftesbury has in mind in this case is philosophical, rather than religious, conceptions about chance.

Student: Does he have a specific group in mind when discussing daemonism?

Teacher: It does not seem so, but he states that some nations are known to worship the devil or a god who is arbitrary and evil.

Student: Why is the question of the order of the world so important for Shaftesbury? If ethics typically concerns interpersonal relations, the question of the order of the world may not seem to have any direct bearing on ethics.

Teacher: This question is central for Shaftesbury because virtue is based on our benevolent affections towards others. In *Sensus Communis*, he also evokes a moral sense which is gradually developed in human society. Shaftesbury in general holds that everything is connected. For him, it is difficult to know a particular substance without knowing its connection to the whole, and each substance has its particular good and interest, as he states in the *Inquiry*.

For Shaftesbury, the good pertains to the substance and also to the whole. It is natural for each substance to have its own particular interest. However, it does not subsist in isolation, and therefore its connection to its surroundings is essential. Moreover, there may not be a conflict between its self-interest and its ability to be good to others. A creature may be said to be good in itself if it is perfect in itself. However, it is said to be good properly if it contributes to the common good.

Student: Returning to the question of religion, how does God become a role model for us, and what influence does that have on human behavior?

Teacher: God is like a role model for human behavior, according to Shaftesbury. If we think of the deity as a benevolent being, then we will also strive to be good. Otherwise, we will not try to act in the best possible way.

Student: When it comes to the emotions, would Shaftesbury agree with Aristotle and Aquinas in saying that the emotions have an important role to play in the practice of virtue?

Teacher: According to Shaftesbury, one is good and virtuous if one is endowed with good and natural affections. One is bad if one does not have those natural and good affections, but rather bad and unnatural affections.

Student: However, one would assume that being good leads to acting on those affections?

Teacher: Yes, being virtuous is based on having natural and good affections, and good actions issue from these good affections, given that virtuous actions are motivated by those affections. Being good or bad comes from one's natural temperament, and virtue represents that goodness in us. An action is judged to be good if it comes from those natural affections, and one's character is good also if it is based on those natural affections. One's motivations also have to be good.

Student: Does Shaftesbury give examples of the natural affections?

Teacher: Some of these affections are love, generosity, gratitude, pity, and helpfulness, and he states that the pleasures afforded by these natural affections are superior to any other kind of human pleasure or inclination.

Student: Are these natural affections innate or do they need to be learned?

Teacher: They are natural in us, but they should be encouraged by mentors and generally by those around us, since they can further develop if one receives a good education.

Student: I understand that Shaftesbury greatly emphasizes the emotions, even more than Aristotle and Aquinas, since virtue is motivated by the emotions more than by an epistemological factor. However, there surely must also be a cognitive aspect to his position on virtue.

Teacher: That is correct, and we have seen that the way we think about the ruling principle of the world does affect our feelings and our behavior. In addition, Shaftesbury speaks of a natural sense of right and wrong.

Student: Is this a natural or a cognitive principle?

Teacher: We could think of it perhaps as both. We have a natural inclination towards the good. If we say that this is a natural sense, it must be inborn rather than acquired later in life. In this sense, Shaftesbury seems to share with Plato in the belief in an innate idea of good. The cognitive element must be assumed because this natural sense of right and wrong allows us to distinguish right from wrong, from a cognitive perspective. Virtue is based on the knowledge of right and wrong as well as on the natural affections.

Student: And this natural sense of right and wrong means that human beings are naturally good?

Teacher: Clearly, that is what Shaftesbury has in mind. He believes that to do good and to be good is the natural human tendency.

Student: And this natural good temperament and affection is related to a sense of right proportion and order?

Teacher: Precisely, and therefore we find a close connection between moral goodness and beauty or aesthetic form. It is all a matter of being able to appreciate what is naturally orderly and proportional.

Student: A good person would then also be able to appreciate art?

Teacher: Yes, there definitely seems to be a connection between ethics and aesthetics in that sense.

Student: However, in the history of art, we know of great artists who were very far from moral perfection, either for crimes that they committed or ideas that they held.

Teacher: That is an important issue, the dissonance between moral and aesthetic perfection, and it deserves a special treatment. We know that philosophers have grappled with that issue, for instance Diderot in *Rameau's Nephew*. It is complex, and perhaps one can find many cases of people whose aesthetic sense is more developed than their moral sense, and vice versa.

Student: Even if that natural sense is present, it can be developed, according to Shaftesbury, can it not?

Teacher: Yes, the legal system, for instance, can promote that natural sense of right and wrong. It is important to have good laws and a sound political system, based on justice, as stressed by Shaftesbury. He himself was actively involved in the politics of his time.

In addition, although ideas about religion do not entirely determine one's natural sense of right and wrong, they can reinforce it or weaken it. The principle of punishment can produce an inclination towards good behavior but the inner motivation for virtue is a stronger factor in producing virtue. A belief in the afterlife also promotes virtue, including a belief in future reward and punishment. Believing in God as a provident benevolent being is also important, because we then view our actions in connection with this benevolent universal order. If we hold that there is no such order or design in the world and in the way particular events happen in the world, then whether our actions are good or not does not seem to matter.

In *Sensus Communis* and *Soliloquy, or Advice to an Author*, Shaftesbury mentions how moral taste develops through education.

Student: There seem to be some similarities between Shaftesbury and Rousseau in the way that they consider human nature to be fundamentally good.

Teacher: Yes, Shaftesbury was extremely influential during the 18th century and it is possible that he influenced Rousseau. However, according to Rousseau, human beings lose their natural goodness once they become part of society, that is to say, once they live in communities, with other human beings. For Shaftesbury, in contrast, it is natural for human beings to want to be in society and meet other human beings, and generally to seek companionship. For Rousseau, human beings are good once they live in nature, and not after human civilization has developed. For Shaftesbury, as for Cicero before him, living with other human beings is natural, and not just for utilitarian purposes. He believes that someone who shuns human society lacks those natural affections and therefore cannot be happy. Such a person is assumed to be generally gloomy and unhappy.

Student: Does that mean that the greatest pleasure comes from being with other human beings?

Teacher: Exactly, that is the outcome of Shaftesbury's theory. He divides pleasure into mental and bodily, and he considers that mental pleasures are superior to bodily pleasures. Within the mental pleasures, he distinguishes between the individual ones and the social ones, and the latter pleasures are preferable. In addition, we also reflect on the natural affections, and this is something good. In general, he holds that the highest pleasures are enjoyed in the context of the natural affections, such as love, generosity and gratitude.

Student: Is there any utilitarian aspect to Shaftesbury's theory of virtue?

Teacher: For Shaftesbury, to be good and virtuous is to benefit others and one's community and to contribute to the common good. In *Sensus Communis* he speaks of a common sense ('sensus communis') consisting in natural notions of morals that are shared by human beings. In that sense, the outcome of an action is important, and there is also a way in which virtue is tied to the benefit to one's community, and in that sense, there is a teleological aspect to virtue and the outcome of virtuous actions and dispositions. However, virtue is just as much about character and intention as about the outcome of the virtuous action, and whether it benefits others.

Student: I understand that the emotions play an important role in Shaftesbury's virtue ethics although the emotions are not dissociated from reason, as we have seen. Are there any similarities with Aristotle's theory of the mean?

Teacher: Shaftesbury believes that emotions should not be excessive. Especially if they are selfish they should not be too strong, and they should have the right objects. At the same time, the natural affections, which are the social affections in the way that they make us help others and enjoy their company, should be firmly rooted in us, like the virtues in Aristotle. In addition, they should be unconditional in the sense that one should not place limits on them. Presumably, these natural affections are ends in themselves, not a means to an end, just like the virtues for Aristotle.

Student: Are there any similarities between Shaftesbury on the one hand, and Socrates and the Stoics on the other, concerning the question of the virtues?

Teacher: That is a pertinent question. For Shaftesbury the natural affections are equivalent to living according to nature and wisdom, and they are also identified with the health of the soul; they are good qualities of the soul, as for the Stoics. It is also important to note that these natural affections are mental qualities. They are related to appetites, and they are natural in the sense that we possess them fundamentally as human beings.

Student: Does that mean that they are not acquired but are natural?

Teacher: Shaftesbury does not mention the process of acquiring the natural affections or the virtues from childhood, but they are rooted in us, and they have an affective and a cognitive aspect. There does not seem to be a strong distinction between cognitive and affective aspects here. Shaftesbury states that the affections are the fundamental roots of the virtues, and this carries with it a distinction between right and wrong. For him, virtue is the right disposition of human beings, as rational creatures, in the matter of objects that are right or wrong.

However, the emphasis on affections is obviously not a Stoic feature—as the Stoic position is described by Cicero in *De finibus*—and neither is the connection between natural affections and virtue. However, for Shaftesbury happiness depends on these natural affections.

Student: I understand that for Shaftesbury the natural affections and the virtues, which issue from the natural affections, can be promoted through politics and education. Presumably the natural affections are naturally exercised when we deal with other people?

Teacher: That is correct, and Shaftesbury also believes that in order to keep one's good temperament and to exercise the natural virtues, it is important to remain occupied, physically and mentally. Obviously, the best kind of exercise consists in exercising our social or natural affections.

Student: Returning to Aquinas, you mentioned that he bases all the passions on love?

Teacher: Yes, and love can be directed toward the good, or toward the person to whom one wishes the good. Regarding the cause of love, he states that the good is the cause of love.

Student: Are there any similarities between Aquinas and Shaftesbury on the question of the good?

Teacher: Shaftesbury, like Aquinas, also seems to be of the opinion that we are naturally attracted to the good, and this is the foundation of the natural affections. To be morally good, for both philosophers, as for Aristotle, consists in being good towards others and our communities and contributing to the common good.

Perhaps another important point in common is the similarity between the good and the beautiful. According to Aquinas, the beautiful and the good are basically the same, only differing in aspect or appearance, as something in which desire or appetite rests. When good is attained, desire or appetite rests in it, and we have seen that appetite is a motive force. In the same way, appetite or desire rests in the beautiful, when it is seen.

Student: Is not the beautiful something physical or resembling the physical, as it is apprehended by the senses?

Teacher: That is an interesting question. In the *Summa Theologiae*, when Aquinas compares the good and the beautiful, he states that the latter is apprehended by the higher senses, namely seeing and hearing, the senses which are closer to reason, by way of serving reason. In addition, they have a stronger cognitive aspect than the other senses, because they furnish more information than the other senses. Aristotle had already stated that we obtain most information through the senses of seeing and hearing. Aquinas remarks that we do not describe tastes or odors as being beautiful. In both cases, of the beautiful and the good, the good pleases the appetite, and the beautiful is pleasant to apprehend.

Student: It appears that the beautiful is not something material, but akin to something spiritual that is apprehended by the mind.

Teacher: Yes. For Aquinas, it seems that the beautiful is associated with the transcendentals, and it constitutes perhaps a combination between that which is sensible, in so far as it is apprehended by the senses, and the spiritual or intellectual, but Aquinas certainly does seem to emphasize the intellectual aspect. For Plato, as we know, the beautiful and the good were intelligible forms, as stated by Socrates in the *Phaedo*. However, Aquinas also distinguishes, in mentioning Aristotle, sensitive love from spiritual love. Seeing leads to knowing and to loving.

Student: Is there also a connection with the true?

Teacher: Yes, in the sense that the good must be known in some way. We love that which we know. However, we do not need to know perfectly that which we love.

Student: I can understand why Aquinas would have to defend that position, given that we ought to know God, even if it is not possible to know perfectly such a perfect being, certainly not in this life.

Teacher: That is right. Aquinas states that the same applies to the sciences, which can be loved even when we do not know them perfectly. However, love causes a greater union between the subject and the object of love, for instance in the case of friendship, than knowledge causes the union between the subject of the knowledge and the object known. And Aquinas follows Augustine in stating that all the emotions of the soul are caused by love.

Student: Could it be argued that love as a passion is something that weakens us, if it makes us become passive rather than active?

Teacher: For Aquinas, love consists in seeking what is good and also what is good for us, and, in that sense, it is something that perfects us instead of weakening us. Naturally Aquinas emphasizes the love of spiritual good. He distinguishes between intelligible pleasure, which pertains to reason and the soul, and physical pleasure, which pertains to the good of the senses. The latter can affect the soul and the body, given the connection between body and soul, and the fact that the soul manages the body. Pleasures of the senses are particularly attached to the body and Aquinas states that concupiscence in particular concerns the sensitive appetite.

Student: And are these two kinds of pleasure connected?

Teacher: They both belong, partly or wholly, to the soul, since the senses serve the sensitive faculty which is part of the soul. Within reason, Aquinas distinguishes between universal and particular reason, the latter being attached to the sensitive part of the soul. And the sensitive appetite can even be moved by universal reason, through particular imagination.

Student: Nevertheless, Aquinas states that spiritual pleasure is greater?

Teacher: Yes, he states that intellectual pleasures are greater, and that knowing through the intellect affords more pleasure than sensible knowledge, the knowledge that is procured by the senses. However, the senses are important because they lead to knowledge and they are also useful. He says that non-rational animals also love the senses for their usefulness in keeping bodily integrity and health. In general, pleasure implies the attainment of some good and the knowledge of that attainment, pleasure being one of the emotions of the soul.

This two-sided aspect of pleasure is natural given that for Aquinas human beings have a rational side and also a sensitive side which is shared with other animals.

Student: In modern philosophy, specifically in philosophers like Descartes and Kant, one tends to think of the emotions, and possibly also pleasure, as possibly constituting an obstacle to reason.

Teacher: That is correct. However, towards the end of *The Passions of the Soul*, Descartes states that the passions are good but should not be misused or go unchecked.

Nevertheless, in contemporary psychology, the line between the emotions and reason has become somewhat blurred, in the sense that there is not a complete separation between emotions and reason but they are found together and they cooperate in our response to many challenges. Phrases like 'emotional intelligence' point to that alliance between reason and the emotions. Perhaps they are different degrees of understanding of reality. Sometimes we sense something but not at a completely conscious level. The emotions may give us important insights in that way, while thinking about the same phenomenon in a rational way takes longer. Sometimes we justify an emotional reaction in a rational way, but the link may be actually already there, and it is simply a case of taking the emotional reaction to another level, rather than changing its nature altogether.

Student: Is there a cognitive aspect to pleasure?

Teacher: Pleasure can be sensitive and intellectual, as we have seen, and in that sense, it presupposes apprehension and it is closely related to knowledge, including sensitive knowledge. With regard to the principle of contact as part of pleasure, Aquinas states that we obtain the greatest pleasure from sensation, hope and memory. The question of conjunction is important because pleasure is caused by the presence of the object loved. And these three sources of pleasure combine direct contact and the possibility of contact. With regard to hope, we wish to obtain the desired object, having the power to do it, and in the case of knowledge we wish to apprehend the object loved, and contact is effected through apprehension. Reason is also present, and it should control the passions of the soul, which are movements of the appetitive power.

Student: Is there a contradiction or tension in Aquinas on the question of pleasure? It seems that the greatest pleasure is intellectual, but perhaps physical pleasure is also distinctly stressed? Perhaps he defends the two kinds of position in the *Summa Theologiae*?

Teacher: If we think of pleasure as contact and in terms of its usefulness for the preservation of life, it appears that physical pleasure is the most important one, but in several passages of the *Summa Theologiae* it is clear that intellectual pleasure is privileged by Aquinas. With regard to the senses, he highlights touch as being the most important of the five senses for preserving animal life. On the other hand, sight is the most important sense for obtaining knowledge.

Student: Is there something to be said for the pleasure obtained in searching for the object of the knowledge?

Teacher: Aquinas states that it is more pleasing to contemplate what we know than to research into what we do not know. However, searching, he states, is sometimes more pleasant.

Student: You have mentioned that the passions have a role to play in the practice of virtue. How does pleasure relate to the virtues, according to Aquinas?

Teacher: Aquinas states, like Aristotle, that it is good and virtuous to take pleasure in good works and in the works of virtue. The virtuous person is the one who takes pleasure in virtuous action. And all this is related to the will. Moral goodness depends mainly on the will. The will moves us to obtain the good, and pleasure, particularly as delight, means to rest in that good. We have also seen that there are different kinds of pleasure and it is important to seek the right kind of pleasure, and that is also virtuous. Naturally, for Aquinas the greatest pleasure consists in the contemplation of the truth.

Student: That would make sense in light of his notion that perfect happiness or beatitude consists in contemplating God, who is also the truth itself.

Teacher: Yes, for him that constitutes the religious and the theological dimension of pleasure and knowledge.

Student: What should we say of the problem of evil in connection with virtue?

Teacher: Evil has many dimensions, as we have seen, but Aquinas subscribes to the Neoplatonic theory of evil as a privation and a lack of good or goodness. There is moral evil, which consists in vice, and when it comes to the passions, we know that the negative passions, like fear and sorrow, involve avoiding some evil. But even the avoidance of evil is prompted by a love of the good, and that is why love is at the root of every passion. According to Aquinas, good is a much more powerful mover than evil, since evil only leads to action for the sake of some good, or perceived good. In any case, reason should command the good, or denounce an evil or injury.

3.2. Habit

Student: We have also seen that habit is an important aspect of virtue and a necessary step in becoming and remaining virtuous.

Teacher: Absolutely—for Aquinas habit is a very important aspect of virtue. After discussing the will and the passions, he examines habit as a preliminary study for the understanding of virtue.

Student: Does he explain the exact meaning of habit?

Teacher: He states that habit comes from the verb to have (from 'habere' in Latin), and that it also means a relation to something else, based on a Latin idiom.

Drawing on Aristotle's *Categories*, he affirms that habit pertains to the category of quality and that it is the first species of quality.

Student: Habit is also closely connected with disposition, is it not?

Teacher: That is correct. Habit is preceded by disposition, and habit implies a certain permanence. Habit, on the one hand, pertains to the nature of something, as a quality, but it also points to action.

Student: How is the quality related to the action?

Teacher: According to Aquinas, who follows Aristotle's position on the issue, habit is considered a first act, or a potentiality to act; when the action is being carried out, it constitutes a second act and realization of the potentiality to act. Habit is like a second nature in the sense that it facilitates action.

Student: This particular distinction between potentiality and act, concerning habit and action, comes from Aristotle's work *On the Soul*?

Teacher: Yes, although the general distinction between actuality and potentiality is also discussed in his *Metaphysics*, as is also the distinction between matter and form.

Student: Aristotle identifies matter with potentiality and form with actuality.

Teacher: Exactly. These terms apply to natural substances that we can find around us, but also to the activity of the soul. If we speak about habit, this distinction refers to the soul, and particularly human beings, especially as Aquinas discusses habit in preparation for the examination of virtue, which is a quality of the soul.

Student: It seems that Aquinas devotes more attention to the question of habit and habituation than does Aristotle.

Teacher: In the *Summa Theologiae*, Aquinas is very systematic in the way he treats most issues. The treatment of habit immediately precedes that of virtue, and he devotes six questions to habit. Before that he dedicates twenty-seven questions to the passions. This is one of the topics on which he expands. Habit is not important simply for acquiring the virtues as the result of repeated virtuous action, but Aquinas also highlights the idea that habit establishes the disposition to act virtuously. It follows from Aristotle's conception of potentiality and actuality, as we have seen. In addition, it is important to stress that other important influences can be found in Aquinas' treatment of the virtues, such as Peter Lombard and Augustine. For instance, Aquinas expands on the question of the cardinal virtues, which are mentioned by Cicero, and then discussed explicitly by other thinkers writing in Latin, including Ambrose, as well as authors in the Platonic or Neoplatonic tradition.

Student: In reading Aquinas, it becomes clear that 'habit' has a different sense for us today than the one it has for Aquinas and for Aristotle before him.

Teacher: Nowadays we tend to think of habit as something almost instinctive or something that we do without thinking, as a reflex. However, it is clear that for Aristotle and for Aquinas, habit is a conscious act and that it belongs to the acts of the mind or the soul.

Student: I understand that virtue issues from habit, but perhaps we could think of virtuous activity as something conscious and intentional without thinking about habit in the same way.

Teacher: In principle, that is possible, and certainly not every passage from potentiality to actuality involves mental activity. However, in the case of human beings that passage in this case implies a process of learning, like writing. In addition, Aquinas also mentions habit in the case of the intellectual virtues, and the connection with consciously intellectual activity is thus buttressed. Habit is also considered a perfection.

Student: Is there a distinction between habit as a more natural or instinctive quality, and habit as rational?

Teacher: Aquinas argues that the sensitive powers can act based on natural instinct, but they can also act as commanded by reason. He gives the example of the imagination, which is considered by him to belong to the powers of sensitive apprehension. However, the habit of first principles, for instance, is in the intellective part of the soul.

Student: Is habit then primarily related to the intellect or to the sensitive power?

Teacher: Aquinas argues that habit is in the will, which is a rational power. In order to justify this position, he states that habit is something that we use when we will. However, he also acknowledges the existence of habit in the sensitive powers, since the sensitive powers need these habits in order to be perfected, in addition to their natural inclinations. Generally speaking, habits, like the virtues, are qualities which inhere in the powers of the soul.

Student: Does not the will tend to be active, contrary to habit?

Teacher: The will, and any appetitive power, according to Aquinas, can move and it can be moved, whereas habit tends to represent a potentiality, which can be actualized and leads to action.

Student: And even habit is a product of action?

Teacher: Yes, for instance in the case of writing. After one learns how to write, writing becomes an acquired habit, which is the true meaning of habit according to Aquinas, such as the possibility of writing for someone who has learned how to write but is not currently writing. It is a potentiality which can be actualized. Habit constitutes a disposition to operation. And it is situated in the powers of the soul.

Student: I understand how habit consists in the development of a disposition which is based on nature. Perhaps there are also natural habits?

Teacher: Habit has to be based on nature, certainly as its starting point. In fact, Aquinas stresses the idea that a good habit disposes the agent to act in conformity with his or her nature. In this sense, habit reinforces nature. And virtue, which constitutes a habit, is also not dissociated from human nature. Rather, it completes nature and perfects it. For Aquinas, and also for the medieval Islamic philosophers, habit is something that is acquired through repetition, and indeed both Aquinas, in Latin, and the medieval Arab philosophers use words for habit that indicate something which has been acquired naturally through practice. We have also seen that some habits pertain to the sensitive powers while others pertain to the intellectual faculties.

Student: Aquinas tends to follow Aristotle on the question of the beginning of knowledge in stating that we first learn through sense perception. Does it mean that habits are primarily related to the sensitive powers?

Teacher: Aquinas holds that we have natural habits which come partly from nature and partly from an extrinsic principle. He also speaks of natural habits in the intellective powers, such as the first principles which cannot be disputed or proved, for instance the principle that the whole is greater than the part. Understanding these first principles constitutes a natural habit.

Student: Are the first principles not like innate ideas, instead of the result of practice?

Teacher: Aquinas states that we first understand what whole and what part is, and then we immediately understand that the whole is greater than the part. The principle itself is obtained through the senses, by seeing whole and parts and relating them to one another. With regard to intellectual habits, Aquinas also says that it is not possible for the intellect to understand several things at the same time, but there is a habit of knowledge for several things, and the intellect, although it is one faculty or power, possesses the powers of several sciences.

Student: And these habits are caused by repetition?

Teacher: Yes, they are caused by repeated acts and the same is true of virtue. Equally, vice becomes ingrained in one's character if evil deeds are repeated. In either case, one act is not sufficient, but repeated action is required. The same goes for the intellectual virtues and the habits of the mind generally. Aquinas states that memory is strengthened by meditation. However, the habits of first principles cannot be forgotten. In addition, the act should be carried out in a careful way in order for virtue to become a habit.

Student: Are there other factors to take into consideration with respect to habit in the way it leads to virtue?

Teacher: The act should be done carefully, as Aquinas says. He adds that habit can be corrupted if the virtuous act ceases to be done. It can also be corrupted by a judgment of reason, ignorance, passion, or deliberate choice.

Student: Should not the person always choose what is best?

Teacher: We can discuss the question of vice and how it is formed in greater detail later, but it is clear that for Aristotle and for Aquinas, vice is not just a question of ignorance. There can be deliberate choice of what is bad.

Student: However, we tend to pursue that which seems good to us.

Teacher: That is right, and therefore this is a complex question.

Student: Aquinas believes that good habits make it easier to perform a virtuous action. In addition, habit concerns many things, if they are interrelated.

Teacher: That is correct.

Student: You mentioned that after examining the nature of habit, Aquinas discusses virtue.

Teacher: Yes, and we will see how he defines virtue, based on the ideas of Aristotle, Cicero, Augustine, and Peter Lombard. Before examining virtue, he had mentioned happiness as the end of virtue, although he privileges happiness in the next life, namely beatitude, as we have seen.

4. The Definition of Virtue

Student: Now that we have discussed the nature of ethics, the place of virtue within ethical theory and the preconditions and goals of ethical and virtuous action, as well as important aspects associated with or leading up to virtue, such as the emotions and the nature of habit, we should discuss the nature and definition of virtue more fully.

Teacher: Yes, we should discuss the meaning of virtue, and the nature of virtue in general before proceeding to the different types of virtue and the individual virtues.

Student: How has virtue been defined by philosophers?

Teacher: In order to understand the definition of virtue, we should keep in mind the special meaning of the Greek term, 'aretē', and also the Latin term, 'virtus', from which 'virtue' in English comes from.

Student: We have seen that virtue pertains to human excellence.

Teacher: Yes, aretē means the role or function or excellence of something. It can apply to human beings but also to inanimate objects. Naturally, with respect to human beings it indicates the rational nature of human beings and also the social and political aspects of human existence and nature, which explains the two kinds of virtue discerned by Aristotle, theoretical and practical.

Student: Does it have the same sense in Plato?

Teacher: It has a similar sense in the way that the virtues bear a moral implication. Although clearly for Socrates virtue is based on knowledge, it really concerns the way we treat one another and the way we live in society. Socrates is interested in investigating human nature, and the way to be good, rather than pursuing other kinds of study, such as the natural sciences.

Student: And there is also the Latin term.

Teacher: Yes, and in Latin virtue points to the notion of 'power'. This is very clear in Aquinas, who frequently mentions Aristotle's definition of virtue in the *On the Heavens* as the limit of power. Later, Spinoza thinks of virtue as being based on one's individual effort of self-preservation.

Student: And does this twofold meaning of virtue still hold today?

Teacher: Virtue concerns the perfection of human nature, even today, in the way it contains several good traits of character, and represents the fulfillment of human nature. In addition, virtue does mean a certain power to act in a certain way. We have seen how virtue is something related to activity, following from human free will and freedom of action.

Student: Spinoza's understanding of virtue as power seems to emphasize our natural rather than our spiritual side.

Teacher: It may seem so initially, given Spinoza's emphasis on the effort, by living things, for self-preservation. It then becomes clear, when we read his *Ethics*, that we are active in so far as we follow our true nature, which in the case of human beings is the understanding or the intellect. If we follow reason we are active and preserve our nature.

Student: It seems that Spinoza's emphasis on desire actually turns into a kind of intellectualism.

Teacher: He associates the passions with our passive and material side, as well as with inconstancy, and hence the need to control them and to focus on having recourse to reason rather than the emotions or passions, as well as the imagination. While reason belongs to us as human beings, the passions reflect the influence of external factors or objects on us, hence the need to control them, that is to say, to control our response to the way in which external objects affect us. For him, virtue consists in acting according to reason.

Student: It seems that, for all his novel ideas, Spinoza very much adheres to Aristotle's understanding of human nature as essentially rational.

Teacher: There is no doubt about that, and he also thinks of the human being as a social animal. He thinks of the emotions as something that belongs to each person in a particular way, while reason is shared by all. He does not share Aristotle's positive view of the emotions and their role in fostering virtuous behavior. He rather takes a Stoic line on the emotions, and he mentions the Stoics explicitly in his *Ethics* as defending the view that reason should control the emotions. These are the root of selfishness and disunity, while reason and virtue are the root of harmony among human beings. In the same way that he believes that virtue is based on following reason, so happiness consists in perfecting reason.

Student: Virtue definitely seems to be a good thing, a good quality to have. Why was it not always the focus of philosophers working in the field of ethics?

Teacher: For a long time, virtue was the focus of philosophers working on ethics, and virtue ethics is now back in fashion. During the period of ancient and medieval philosophy ethics was centered on virtue ethics, as we know from studying Plato, Aristotle, and the Hellenistic and medieval philosophers. Even in the modern period, virtue was the focus of attention of various philosophers, in particular British philosophers, like Hume and Shaftesbury. It seemed natural to think of ethics as based on the notion of personal virtue, without disregard for more communal kinds of virtue, such as justice. For a more structural treatment of ethical action, politics seemed to be the right discipline for debating those questions.

Virtue became less appealing later when other ethics models came to prevail, for instance with Kant's duty ethics, which focuses on universal rules for all subjects. Perhaps the association of virtue with some perceived shortcomings of virtue ethics, such as the need for the development of an individual's character, variations in virtuous practice from person to person, the association of virtue with the emotions, and the difficulty of defining virtue, made virtue ethics less appealing. Even so, we can find a focus on virtue in Schopenhauer and later philosophers, so perhaps it was never truly out of fashion. Some scholars might even associate virtue with the kind of morality which was prevalent during Victorian Britain, which is the better part of the 19th century.

Student: However, for some scholars and philosophers, virtue could not represent all of ethics, since other approaches seemed more plausible or successful.

Teacher: Yes, perhaps there were some shortcomings in some theories of virtue. We have seen how Aristotle thinks of virtue or perfect virtue as achievable possibly only by adult male citizens, to the exclusion of women or slaves. However, we have seen that Plato upholds a different kind of virtue ethics, which is based on the principle that virtue is the same in man, woman, child and slave.

Student: There is also the problem of particularism and the way in which virtue can vary from person to person, as well as among different groups of people, and in different regions, according to Aristotle.

Teacher: Yes, but again, this would not be a problem for Plato, who thinks of the virtues as forms. In that sense, they would not change according to circumstances, and they would not vary from place to place. In addition, in Aristotle, virtue is measured by the virtuous man, and perhaps we could ask ourselves whether good men prompt in us the definition of virtue or whether virtue makes the virtuous person.

Student: We have seen that Aristotle, in his metaphysics, starts from particular things or substances, and he appears to follow a similar method in his ethics.

Teacher: Absolutely. For Aristotle, the starting point for knowledge and philosophical study, generally speaking, lies in particular things which we observe and study. Virtue is at the center of his ethics, and in that case too we learn about ethics from virtuous people, in particular adult men, who can develop freely and are not hampered by the political and perhaps also the natural limitations which beset women and slaves in ancient Greece.

Student: But Aristotle also privileges the universal, for instance when he argues that true knowledge is of the universal and not of particular things.

Teacher: Exactly, and perhaps the same can be said of the virtues. Even if one starts off with an impressive particular model for the virtues, in the end general rules about virtue and the particular virtues must be found. For instance, Aristotle defines virtue as a golden mean between two extremes, and this can provide guidance as to virtuous behavior in particular circumstances.

Student: This seems to be another criticism of virtue ethics, its inability to provide universal rules of conduct.

Teacher: Yes, whereas Kant, for instance, states that always telling the truth is an absolute principle.

Student: There seems to be a certain tension between the kind of ethics that provides general principles and the kind of virtue ethics which states that circumstances must be taken into account.

Teacher: That may be, but one could point out possible shortcomings in each of the approaches, whether universalist or particularist, especially at the time of implementation. A universalist approach focusing on putting general rules into practice, in particular cases, could present difficulties, while a particularist approach could lack clarity, given the need to assess particular situations. Perhaps a combination of both would be the ideal position—in other words, general principles of the virtues that can be adapted according to particular circumstances.

In the end the best course of action ought to be chosen, and perhaps carefully taking into account the circumstances is the best way forward.

Student: The Stoics also seem to stand for a universalist conception of the virtues, is that so?

Teacher: Yes, there is one model for everyone and this is the wise man, as stressed by the Stoics, for instance Seneca. This does not vary according to circumstances, and the wise man is impervious, in his behavior, to the reverses of fortune.

Student: There seems to be a tension between the notion of ethics as prescriptive, like Kantian ethics, and a kind of ethics that contemplates different models of implementation.

Teacher: That is correct, and scholars think of virtue ethics as part of normative ethics, like utilitarianism and duty ethics, since it views ethics in its capacity to prescribe and recommend, as opposed, for instance, to metaethics, which studies broader questions, like the concept of value. Ethics describes an ideal behavior which should become the goal of human action.

Student: We have seen that disciplines like bioethics have that ability to turn into something practical.

Teacher: Yes, through that kind of ethical reflection policy makers can adopt particular measures and laws.

Student: A particularist approach to ethics could mean that different conceptions of virtue exist in different parts of the world.

Teacher: We know that according to Aristotle, unlike for Plato, ethics is not a precise science, which means that there can be adjustments according to the circumstances and the people involved, in addition to the differences in time and place. Perhaps it is also possible to find commonalities in spite of these differences. These differences may not pose a threat to virtue, broadly conceived, as a valid approach in ethics.

Student: With regard to the difference between duty ethics and virtue ethics, some scholars have argued that duty ethics is more aligned with the principle of a universal law, which would not be the case for virtue ethics, in the sense that law obliges and virtue merely recommends and is not binding. We could also think of law as something that is imposed from outside or above, although it can be internalized, while virtue develops from within. However, virtue requires models, and therefore it cannot be a purely particular affair.

Teacher: It can also be argued that that difference between virtue and law was bridged in the Middle Ages, when we find a strong presence of virtue ethics, but also the notion of a universal law giver, namely God, alongside fundamental rules of action that are binding, such as the Ten Commandments.

Student: Is this also observable in Aquinas?

Teacher: Aquinas develops the kind of virtue ethics proposed by Aristotle. We have seen that virtue ethics can take on different shapes, and this is immediately observable in the differences between Plato and Aristotle. In Aquinas, who follows Aristotle's approach, this kind of ethics does not clash with a strong view of universal principles such as the laws, by intertwining questions of individual character and the way it should develop, with the abidance of the law. In addressing the connection between virtue and law in the *Summa Theologiae*, Aquinas argues that acting virtuously involves habit, whereas the law does not necessarily presuppose habit. In that sense, the law does not punish one for the lack of certain virtues, although it certainly encourages virtuous behavior.

In Aquinas we also find a connection between the natural law and the virtues. It is clear that, at least in the medieval and the modern period, virtue is expected of everyone without exception.

Student: And the Stoics also have a universalist view of virtue?

Teacher: Absolutely. In that sense we can argue that a particularistic approach is characteristic of Aristotle's account of virtue, in the way that there can be variations in the applications of the various virtues. And since Aristotle articulates ethics and politics, particularistic does not mean a relativistic approach to ethics.

Student: What about Roman philosophers, and their approach to this question?

Teacher: Cicero adopts important aspects of the Stoic theory of virtue as the only true good. At the same time, he also accepts the Platonic view of the four main virtues, and many aspects of Aristotle's view on friendship, which is an important virtue.

Student: His position seems very eclectic.

Teacher: Yes, Cicero claims that he does not follow any particular school, but chooses the school which seems the best one to him according to the subject matter at hand. Seneca in turn embraces the Stoic theory of virtue, exemplified by the Stoic wise man.

Student: Is the ideal of the Stoic wise man easily achievable?

Teacher: No, it is very difficult, and Seneca himself admits that he has not reached that ideal, although he strives to achieve it.

Student: There seem to be many kinds of virtue ethics, or rather different approaches to virtue.

Teacher: Exactly, and virtue never really went out of fashion, in spite of a different approach advanced by Kant, who himself writes about virtue. In addition, it is possible to combine virtue ethics with other approaches. A contemporary philosopher, Julia Driver, argues for a consequentialist interpretation of virtue ethics.

Student: We have looked into the preconditions of ethics, namely the need for moral action to be voluntary and not by force or done in ignorance. In addition, moral action involves decision and it concerns the good and the bad. Furthermore, the goal as well as the means are important and the subject of the action must also be taken into account.

Teacher: Yes, virtuous action is typically human and performed between human beings.

Student: We have looked into common aspects between moral action and virtuous action.

Teacher: Yes, virtuous action is also voluntary, it implies a decision and the choice between good and bad. It establishes a goal and the choice of the means is also important. The human subject and the object of the action are important aspects of virtuous action. That is only to be expected, since virtue ethics is a subset of ethics.

Student: In order to see what is specific to virtue ethics it would be good to return to the definition of virtue.

Teacher: Yes, let us return to the definition of virtue, or rather the definitions of virtue.

Student: We have discussed the etymological sense of the term, as meaning primarily 'excellence' in ancient Greek and 'power' in Latin.

Teacher: Yes, and the variations in the meaning of virtue influence the way different philosophers define virtue. Plato has a certain understanding of virtue, and Aristotle has his own definition. In the Middle Ages, Augustine defines virtue in a certain way, and this is taken up by Aquinas. In the modern period, there are other definitions of virtue, provided by Shaftesbury and Hume, for example.

Student: And for Plato, virtue is a kind of harmony of the soul, which allows the soul to rule over the body.

Teacher: That is true. The harmony of the soul is the fundamental meaning of virtue for Plato. The notion that virtue is something in the soul and is a good quality of the soul which then translates into action is present in Plato's works, and Socrates defends it in the Platonic dialogues.

Student: Does Aristotle have a more complex understanding of virtue?

Teacher: Aristotle certainly offers a more systematic treatment of virtue, although he builds on Plato's conception of virtue. Like Plato, Aristotle argues that virtue is a quality that is to be found in the soul as a positive quality. It is particularly associated with the intellect for both philosophers. However, we have seen that it also involves wish or desire, and the notion of a goal or final cause.

Student: Aristotle has a specific definition, correct?

Teacher: That is right; he understands virtue as a mean between two extremes. For instance, courage is the mean between cowardice and foolhardiness.

Student: Aristotle seems to be fond of finding a mean in opposing theories.

Teacher: Yes, hence our expression 'the golden mean', or the mean as the desirable position between two extremes.

Student: Aristotle also allows for the presence of emotion in practicing virtue, as we have seen.

Teacher: Certainly, that is a central element within Aristotle's theory of virtue, the fact that feeling or emotion is part of virtuous action. In particular, one should feel pleasure in doing good deeds and acting virtuously. Otherwise, one is not perfectly virtuous.

Student: This is related to the fact that Aristotle views virtue as something natural, as we have seen.

Teacher: Precisely. Virtue follows nature, and pleasure in this sense indicates that one is following nature, since pleasure signals the completion of human nature. Virtue is the perfection and fulfillment of human nature, and pleasure is the sign of the agreement between human nature and virtue.

Student: In that sense, someone who is indifferent towards virtue, or finds it difficult to act virtuously, has some way to go to perfect virtue?

Teacher: Yes, because that can indicate a tendency or disposition to do the opposite of virtuous action, namely, something vicious.

Student: Is it possible to think of a neutral action in this case, an action that is not good or evil?

Teacher: This is a very interesting question, in the sense that virtue is a choice between good and evil, more specifically the choice of good over evil, obviously. In that sense, a neutral action does not seem to be an ethical action; in other words, it does not make a morally good or detrimental impact on others. In that sense, the virtuous action is also the choice of something good, and ethical action in general is always about good and evil. It cannot be morally neutral.

There is also the question of the connection between virtue and duty. Does virtue mean to do something that we are supposed to do in any case, or it is something over and above duty?

Student: Do you refer to whether virtue is something obligatory or just something over and above normal human action, like a supererogatory action?

Teacher: In the sense that virtue involves the choice of a good action, and that ethical actions are not neutral, then being good implies being virtuous. Obviously, some people are more virtuous than others. Aquinas defended the idea that people participate differently in virtue. There are naturally degrees of virtue, and it cannot be a question of one's being either the Stoic wise man or not virtuous at all. There must be something in between complete virtue and no virtue at all. Each of us is expected to be good and virtuous, even if we cannot attain complete virtue. It is not clear how one could forsake virtue completely, especially if we have in mind the moral virtues, which are the ones that first come to mind when we think of the virtues.

Student: I agree that complete virtue cannot be expected of the majority of people, and that basic virtuous action has the character of something that is obligatory or at least expected.

Teacher: We can debate the role of virtue within the wider questions of good and right, more specifically how virtue relates to what constitutes doing what is good and doing the right thing.

Student: And the notion of right is more closely related to the concept of law and legal principles?

Teacher: Yes, and these questions are always present, just like the theme of the links between ethics and politics or virtue and politics.

Student: We could also think of duties and their connection with virtue.

Teacher: There is a conceptual distinction between duty and virtue. Something done out of duty is obviously good, and it is also virtuous, especially if it comes from a virtuous person who habitually acts in a virtuous way. It seems that every duty we fulfill, like helping relatives and friends, is virtuous, in the sense that it is good and that it benefits others. The terms 'virtue', 'duty', 'good' and 'right' are certainly related.

Student: Is virtuous action about doing what is good or simply what is right?

Teacher: Virtuous action is right, since it is good, but perhaps the question remains of the relation between obligatory action and supererogatory action.

Student: That distinction might not be easily defined, given that sometimes the virtuous deed is the right thing to do and also something good.

Teacher: Yes, even when the right course of action seems like the only option open to us. What is right appears to be a duty that has to be performed. If we think of the right thing to do, then it is the only acceptable option. The right thing to do tends to be a duty, even when it is not formally acknowledged as such. A virtuous action is good, but the fact that it is virtuous does not imply that it is a duty or an obligation, as something imposed from outside, but it must come from the subject.

Nevertheless, if we think of right and good in a general sense, there is not much difference in practical terms. It is good to help people who need us, and it is also the right thing to do, and one could add that this would also indicate a duty. Right and virtuous action are both good, but good seems to be the more general term. What is right seems a more objective or external measure for judging action, while virtue can take more nuanced overtones, concerning the subject of the action and the circumstances involved.

Student: In any case the virtuous person would do what is right, correct?

Teacher: Yes, for instance, the courageous or just person would help those in need.

Student: It does seem like virtue leaves us with more options in terms of the kind of action that is to be performed. The right thing to do seems to be the only correct or acceptable option, whereas virtue allows for more possibilities?

Teacher: Yes, in that sense, the right thing to do and our duty is always something virtuous, but virtue could go beyond duty.

Student: And the right thing to do goes hand in hand with duty?

Teacher: The concepts of right and duty are closely aligned, as we have seen, whereas virtue includes what is right but goes beyond it, or in any case it allows for going beyond the call of duty.

Student: In that sense, that kind of virtuous action is to be praised, but one cannot be blamed for not undertaking it?

Teacher: That is correct. And sometimes doing one's duty, although it is meritorious, is not as highly valued as going beyond the call of duty.

Student: Perhaps you could provide an example?

Teacher: Sure. Loving others or being good to others, that which is called benevolence and which features particularly in the writings of modern philosophers, and specifically modern British philosophers, is a virtue. It is also tied to friendship. Benevolence or love of others implies that we help others. In the Gospel of John, Jesus says that there is no greater love than to give one's life for one's friends. That is the height of friendship and love for our friends, it is the supreme example of the virtue of friendship. It is obviously admirable, but not a duty or a law, or something that is usually expected of us. This would be a case of exemplary or perfect virtue.

Student: I understand that there are degrees of virtue, for instance from helping others to giving one's life for others. It would be good to learn more about friendship later.

Teacher: Friendship has a special place in the works of ancient philosophers. Plato writes about friendship, as does Aristotle, and later Cicero. Aristotle states that friendship is a virtue or at least accompanies virtue. Again, it is something desirable and expected, but it is not something obligatory, unless it is understood in the general sense of benevolence and wishing others well, in addition to helping them when necessary.

Student: The notion of good is always involved in these actions, whether they are virtuous, right, or simply a duty?

Teacher: Yes, they are all part of ethical actions which make other peoples' lives better in some way. Again, we tend to think of virtue primarily as moral virtue, or virtue of character, but the intellectual virtues are also extremely important, and they are not completely separate from the moral virtues. Aquinas states, in his *Commentary on the* Nicomachean Ethics, that the moral virtues predispose us to the intellectual virtues. We will spend more time on the intellectual virtues later.

Student: We have seen how virtue implies a choice of the good, and it is something that resides in the soul or in the mind. For Aristotle it is a mean between two extremes and it involves the emotions. It also follows reason. Are there other aspects of Aristotle's definition of virtue which we should take into account in this context?

Teacher: For Aristotle, the circumstances surrounding an action are also extremely important. In that sense, correct judgment is central to the outcome of the virtuous action.

Student: But is virtue about the outcome of an action or rather about the virtuous or good quality of the agent?

Teacher: The virtuous action is the action done by someone virtuous, so it is inextricably tied to the agent, and this is clear in Aristotle's works. However, and although we are very far from a utilitarian conception of ethics in this case, the outcome is important in the sense that if it is not good, it means that perhaps the circumstances were not taken into account or correctly assessed.

Student: What are these particular circumstances?

Teacher: These are the circumstances of the action, and in that sense virtue is the action done by the virtuous person but the action itself can be considered virtuous or not. The virtuous action should be done at the right time, concerning the right things, towards the right objects or people, and it should be for the right end, and done in the right way.

Student: Perhaps we should analyze these elements in detail.

Teacher: Yes, since these elements encapsulate Aristotle's theory of virtuous action. When we think of the right time for a virtuous action it could be, for instance, to help others when they need us, instead of letting the time of need pass. If we think of the right things, we could think of the kind of help to be provided, for instance, whether material or spiritual. The right people should also be taken into account, in this case those most in need of our help. The right end should also be aimed at. One should not help others, for example, in order to become famous, but for their own benefit. This should be done in the right way, so helping others by our own means, and not, for instance, by stealing.

Student: Virtuous action seems to be a matter of precision.

Teacher: Yes, and consequently virtue requires preparation and also various mental acts, such as deliberation and judgment. In this context, we can understand where the intellectual virtues come into play, since moral virtue requires knowledge. A virtuous action, such as a wise or prudent action, involves deliberation about the means and judgment about the particular action which should be done. In the *Summa Theologica*, Aquinas states that judgment is also an act of justice, and that it constitutes a right decision regarding that which is just.

Student: I understand the complexity of a virtuous action, and all the different elements required of the agent as well as the right elements. It seems that virtue is primarily a matter of benefiting others rather than ourselves?

Teacher: Virtue in general, particularly the moral virtues, is directed to the good of others, given that virtue as part of ethics concerns the way we treat others, and pertains to justice, for instance, and may involve courage or fortitude. However, certain virtues concern the way we treat ourselves, like temperance, which broadly means self-control.

Student: Returning to the definition of virtue, other philosophers offered other definitions of virtue, did they not?

Teacher: Yes, in the medieval period other definitions of virtue emerge. For instance, Aquinas states that virtue is the good use of the will. For him, virtue can reside in the intellect, but moral virtue is in the appetitive part of the soul, or in the appetite. As we have seen, these two faculties, the intellect and the appetite or will, which is rational appetite, are closely allied. The object of the intellect is the truth and the object of the will is the good, and the action of the will implies motion. Naturally, in acting virtuously, the end goal must be some good.

Student: Does Aquinas also have a complete definition of virtue, which takes into account previous definitions, like those of Saint Augustine?

Teacher: Absolutely. Aquinas states that virtue is a habit, in particular an operative habit, and also a perfection of power. It pertains to the soul and the works it produces are good. Virtue cannot be misused and through virtue we live righteously. He also states, following Aristotle, that virtue is the disposition of something perfect to that which is best. In the *Disputed Questions on Virtue*, he states that virtue consists in the fulfillment of a capacity.

Following Augustine, he also says that virtue consists in the correct use of free will. And, following Aristotle, he states that virtue is a disposition to what is best, and that the virtue of a thing makes its work good.

Student: When he says that virtue is a perfection of a power this can also mean a faculty, correct?

Teacher: Yes, and in particular, virtuous action involves reason. Aquinas also states in this context that power refers to being and acting, since power can also mean potentiality. In particular, virtue makes one good and also makes one's act good. For Aquinas, virtue is an operative habit.

Student: We should analyze this definition in more detail.

Teacher: Undoubtedly, it is a very complete and informative definition.

Student: The definition offered by Aquinas shares some elements of the previous definition by Aristotle, namely, the fact that it is a habit and that it resides in the soul.

Teacher: That is right. Habit is central because for Aristotle, virtue is not just about knowledge but requires continued practice and in that sense it is a very practical concern. For him, virtue is in the soul, as we have seen, because it involves knowledge and the intellect as well as the will, or wish. For Aquinas, virtue belongs to the soul, and not to the body.

Student: And for Plato virtue was also a positive quality of the soul.

Teacher: Exactly. However, since for Socrates, virtue is a matter of knowledge, perhaps in order to practice virtue only knowledge is required, rather than long practice.

Student: I understand. Aquinas also mentions the fact that it is a perfection of power.

Teacher: We have seen that this conception of virtue is associated with the Latin term used for virtue, which points to power and strength. In this sense, we have the power to act, and virtue is part of that power, as free will is also. Aquinas thinks of virtue as an act instead of being. This statement resembles Aristotle's understanding of virtue not as state but as activity. In addition, Aquinas follows Aristotle in affirming that the virtue of something makes what it produces good. Virtue is also a principle of operation, as well as an ordered disposition in the soul. On the one hand, virtue reflects the disposition and nature of the agent, but it also makes the agent who possesses it good, and in that way, it is a principle of action and also an end goal. Virtue is always said with reference to good, in so far as it is the limit of a power, whereas evil denotes the lack of something.

Student: We have seen that virtue is a habit.

Teacher: A habit, as we have seen, is something that is acquired through practice and repetition. It is a quality that becomes an acquisition, which makes a virtuous action easier to perform. This has a particular meaning for Aristotelian philosophers, in the sense that habit is an actualized ability to do something, even if we are not constantly doing it. For Aquinas, habit gives one the aptitude to act and also the right use of that aptitude.

Student: It is like being able to write after learning how to write, as we have seen.

Teacher: Exactly. Writing requires practice, and then it becomes something acquired. However, Aristotle stresses the fact that virtue is something active, and this is also true for Aquinas. Virtue can be a state in the sense that the virtuous person has the virtues even if he or she is not practicing them, but it is not primarily a state, or a capacity, even if it presupposes a capacity, and it is not feeling or emotion.

Student: And probably that is why children cannot be considered to be perfectly virtuous?

Teacher: This may have to do with the fact that it takes time to acquire the virtues, and also the knowledge that enables the practice of the virtues. One should bear in mind that for Aquinas, for instance, a child is considered to have attained the age of reason around the age of seven, which is quite early, although that may be the beginning of a continuous practice of virtue or at least of certain virtues. Perhaps some virtues are easier to acquire at different ages.

Student: Is the acquisition process finished upon reaching adulthood?

Teacher: Virtue must keep being practiced, and this belongs to the practical nature of virtue. Moreover, someone who does not practice the virtues cannot be considered virtuous.

Student: That makes perfect sense. I believe that contemporary psychology also confirms this point, namely that practicing the virtues makes us better at the virtues, for instance in the case of temperance.

If all virtues require continuous practice, is that also the case for the process of knowledge, and the intellectual virtues?

Teacher: That is correct; the learning process must be a lifelong process.

Student: Aquinas also says that virtue produces good works; is this a condition of virtuous action?

Teacher: We have highlighted a fundamental difference between virtue ethics and utilitarianism, in the sense that virtue takes account of everything, namely, the nature of the agent, the goal she sets herself, and the object of the action, in addition to the circumstances, and the means to the end. This is a more complete account of ethical action than we find in utilitarianism, which privileges the end result of the action, rather than the agent and the means used to attain that end. However, if we take all these factors into account, then the end result should be a good work, and a good result.

Student: If it is not a good work, perhaps some circumstance was not taken care of?

Teacher: Yes, our action may not be perfectly virtuous if we help people who do not need it, or if we do not help the people who are most in need of us. An example of virtuous action could include giving to charity and to those who are most in need, which will result in a good outcome. We can think of many possible combinations where one of the factors is neglected or not perfectly known.

The general requirements for virtue mean that the subject of the action must be good and aim towards the good, as we have seen, and the intervening circumstances should be evaluated.

Student: Does virtuous action always produce good works?

Teacher: If all the elements that go into virtuous action are considered and the requirements are in place, then there should be a good effect. It could be said that the goal of virtue is to help others and to contribute to communal life. It also leads to the result of helping ourselves in the sense that we become better persons.

Student: To say that by virtue we live righteously means to say that we become better?

Teacher: Yes, by virtue we perfect ourselves. Virtue always requires habit and practice. The conception of virtue as living righteously is championed by several philosophers.

Student: Is it true that virtue cannot be misused?

Teacher: In the *Summa Theologiae*, Aquinas states that one can think badly of virtue and one may wish to avoid it, but when it is practiced it does not produce bad effects.

Student: Could a person not be too generous, so as to become poor, or give to someone who is going to misuse the amount we give them?

Teacher: Virtue requires not just practice but also good judgment and deliberation, and therefore, we should ensure that we are acquainted with the circumstances before we undertake the virtuous action.

Student: Is the virtuous action judged on the basis of the results?

Teacher: As we have seen, virtue is a quality of the soul, and it requires practice. Consequently, the agent must be in the right disposition of mind in addition to choosing and using the right means for the right goal, and assessing the circumstances.

Student: With regard to the misuse of virtue, could one not be, for instance, too courageous, so as to put oneself in danger, while perhaps not helping others in that process?

Teacher: In that case, the person is likely being foolhardy instead of courageous. The question of the golden mean is important but it is also complex. It is clear that Aristotle thinks of the mean not as a universal mathematical principle, but as a reference that should be fixed with regard to the agent and the circumstances. This means that the mean is not the same for everyone; it could change and be adjusted. In some cases, perhaps virtue could be seen as an excess, if someone gives one's life for others, for instance, in the context of a war, but still virtue could not be misused. To misuse virtue would mean to use it for a non-virtuous end, while virtue seems to be an end in itself.

Student: Perhaps it could be misused unintentionally?

Teacher: Virtue is something good which should produce good effects. The end goal of virtue is good and the agent is good, acting with good intentions. Virtue is a good in itself and it serves a good purpose. In addition, virtue does not truly seem to be a means to something, but an end in itself. In that sense, it cannot be misused, otherwise it would cease to constitute virtue. The fact that virtue is aligned with the good, which is an end in itself, means that virtue cannot be misused. Aquinas also states that one could be proud of being virtuous, or one could hate virtue or think ill of it, but one cannot misuse virtue as an operative habit or a principle of action. An act of virtue cannot be evil, it is always good.

Student: Is it possible for a non-virtuous person to perform a virtuous action?

Teacher: In principle, that is possible. We have seen that it is difficult to be completely virtuous. At the same time, a philosopher like Shaftesbury states that it is very difficult to find someone completely bad.

There are also degrees of virtuousness in people and a virtuous action can be the start of a process of becoming virtuous. Virtue requires habit, and practicing virtuous actions leads to a virtuous character, which in turn makes it easier to practice good deeds.

Student: Philosophers such as Plato, Aristotle, Augustine and Aquinas state that virtue is in the soul. Already Plato makes distinctions among the different functions or faculties of the soul, and Aristotle elaborates on that point. Some faculties are closer to the body and others are more abstract. Sensation is part of the soul, as are memory and intellect.

Teacher: For the purposes of virtue, Aristotle states that the soul includes a rational and a nonrational part. With regard to the nonrational part, Aristotle states that virtue is not in the nutritive part, by which plants and animals digest food and grow. He further mentions the motive or motor part of the soul, which includes appetite and desire, and which can be aligned with reason, in the way it listens to reason. Within the rational part we find the will according to Aquinas, in his interpretation of Aristotle's position.

Student: If I understand it correctly, there are two parts of the soul in connection with virtue, one which is nonrational but which listens to reason and the other which is rational. That is to say, one part, the motive part within the nonrational part, listens to reason, while the will is within the rational part of the soul and naturally follows reason. Each of the parts which listens to reason or is aligned with reason is capable of virtue.

Teacher: Yes, this distinction between the rational part and the part which listens to reason corresponds broadly to the division between the types of virtues. The virtues of thought issue from the rational part of the soul, such as wisdom, comprehension and prudence, whereas generosity and temperance are virtues of character and concern the appetitive part of the soul in so far as it obeys reason. Virtue is a good quality of the soul that is praiseworthy. The role of reason is important in the sense that virtue, as we see here, implies always listening to reason, as Aquinas also states, following Aristotle.

Student: Naturally, this is an important point regarding virtue. The way in which we consider virtue and the different kinds of virtue depend on its location within the soul and the connections between virtue and the different parts of the soul.

Teacher: Yes, and the philosophers make distinctions as to where exactly virtue is in the soul. Wish or will is associated with the rational part of the soul, but a full-fledged theory of the will in the way we understand it, as a wish that is closely associated with reason, leading to rational choice, comes with Augustine, who identifies the self or our consciousness of our actions with the will.

Student: Aquinas also elaborates on Aristotle's understanding of virtue, both with regard to the definition of virtue and the connections between virtue and the soul, correct?

Teacher: Yes, Aquinas develops his theory of virtue in various works, and in the *Summa Theologiae* he offers a detailed treatment of virtue, as part of his treatment of human nature. In it he analyzes the various elements that go hand in hand with virtue, such as the nature of habit and the nature of the passions, as we have seen, before analyzing virtue properly so called. He examines the definition of virtue and then states where virtue is in the soul.

The Scholastic philosophers tend to be very systematic and they use Aristotelian concepts to structure their analysis, as we have seen. According to Aquinas, each virtue must inhere in only one power or faculty of the soul. And whereas knowledge is required in the case of moral virtue, moral virtue must be allocated to the appetitive part of the soul, and therefore it is essentially in the appetite. Aquinas further states that virtue is also in the will, which consists in rational appetite. Prudence, for instance, establishes a bridge between the appetite and the intellect, in the way its subject is the practical intellect while it presupposes the rectitude of the will. In this way, the moral virtues subsist in the appetitive part of the soul, whereas the intellectual virtues are in the intellect, like science, wisdom and understanding or comprehension.

A further distinction can be made between speculative intellect and the practical intellect, and Aquinas specifies, as we have seen, that practical intellect is the subject of prudence. Prudence has a theoretical and a practical side. For Aquinas it is an intellectual virtue that has much in common with the moral virtues, since it consists in right reason about the things that are to be done. When it comes to the moral virtues, they reside in different powers of the soul. Fortitude or courage is attributed to the irascible power, whereas temperance is ascribed to the concupiscible power, which means that they are not in the rational part of the soul. These two powers are the two parts of the sensitive appetite, and they obey reason.

Student: There seems to be a distinction among the moral virtues as to their location within the faculties of the soul.

Teacher: Yes, because Aquinas states explicitly that justice is in the will, while temperance and courage are respectively in the concupiscible and the irascible parts of the soul.

Student: Perhaps there are other differences between the practical and the theoretical intellect?

Teacher: The theoretical intellect is purely rational in itself and in its activity, while the practical intellect is applied to other parts of the soul and human spheres of activity, as Aquinas states in his commentary on Aristotle's *Nicomachean Ethics*.

Student: Is there perhaps a certain ambiguity in Aquinas' treatment of the subject of the virtues in the *Summa Theologica* in what concerns the intersection between the practical and the theoretical intellect?

Teacher: At one point, Aquinas states that prudence belongs in reason, which he goes on to describe as theoretical intellect, but he also identifies prudence with the practical intellect. As for the moral virtues, they generally go along with reason, but they also seem to subsist in nonrational parts of the soul, like temperance and courage. However, the ambiguity goes back to Aristotle, who also says that virtue is not in the nonrational parts of the soul, but then admits that courage and temperance are in the nonrational parts of the soul.

In seeking to expand on Aristotle's theory and to be more precise, Aquinas also expands on the ambiguity. However, it is clear that reason is the measure of virtue, and that virtue means that these parts of the soul which are not in the intellect obey reason willingly. Aquinas adds that there can be virtue in the imagination, cogitation and memory, since these powers obey reason. In the case of the moral virtues, there must be a connection with reason, even if they reside in the non-rational parts of the soul, and the connection with reason is even clearer with the intellectual virtues, as we shall see.

Student: Perhaps this ambiguity and the role of the non-rational aspects in virtue has something to do with the emotions or passions?

Teacher: Yes, both Aristotle and Aquinas are keen on integrating the emotional aspects of human nature into their theories of virtue, hence the inclusion of nonrational parts of the soul. This would not be the case for Plato, or the Stoics. Cicero, for instance, defines virtue as a habit that follows nature and is in keeping with reason. For Cicero, then, virtue is part of human nature, or rather a development of it, while reason remains a central aspect of virtuous action. In this respect, Aquinas underscores the fact that the irascible and concupiscible powers are the subject of human virtue in so far as they participate in reason. Interestingly, he adds that these powers do not obey reason automatically, in the way that the body obeys the soul; rather, they have their own way or inclination. The sensitive appetite can help or hinder the rational appetite, which is the will.

Student: Aquinas, as you mentioned, expands on the role of the will, in relation to Aristotle, and he understands it as rational appetite.

Teacher: That is correct. For medieval philosophers, there are different kinds of appetite or desire, some of which are more closely connected with reason or intellect while others are more closely associated with the senses or more basic faculties of the soul. In that sense, the will, and appetite more broadly understood, is a very complex faculty or power for medieval philosophers.

Alfarabi, for instance, in *The Principles of the Opinions of the Inhabitants of the Virtuous City*, understands appetite or desire as a faculty that is present already at the level of the senses, while accepting that it is also associated with other faculties, including the imagination and reason. It is essentially a kind of inclination, but is also explains an attitude of repugnance or avoidance in us, and in that way, it applies to the objects of the other faculties. The will is akin to the appetite. The use of that faculty ensures that human action is good or not; in other words, an action is only considered good or evil if it involves this faculty.

In his works, Aristotle refers to desire, commenting on how living beings seek and avoid certain things. We know that this faculty was further examined by medieval philosophers, in particular Augustine and Aquinas, as well as by later philosophers. The will obviously plays a central role in ethical theory, since it grounds voluntary action, on the one hand, and, on the other, it ensures that the agent can be held responsible for an action.

Student: Aquinas treats this faculty in a systematic way?

Teacher: Yes, in the *Summa Theologiae*, he states that the will concerns the end, while choice concerns the means. Aquinas considers other forms of appetite, like natural appetite and the sensible appetite. The will is connected to the intellect in the way that it consists in an inclination which follows a form that has been understood. On the other hand, the intellect understands the act of the will, and the intellect moves the will with regard to the determination of the act, which comes from the object of the act. In turn, the will moves the intellect with respect to exercising the act. He also argues that for Aristotle, the will is in reason. Aquinas holds that the will can follow the passions or resist them. As we have seen, there is a distinction between the will and the choice of the means, which is the role of prudence. Reason, through the virtue of prudence, chooses the methods, while the will aims at the end. A good action also implies that the affections are inclined to the good. Naturally the term 'prudence' is used by Aristotle and Aquinas in a broader way than it is today. For instance, for Aquinas caution is only a part of prudence, and to be prudent does not mean solely to be cautious.

Student: I understand. Do all faculties of the soul potentially obey reason and receive virtue?

Teacher: Aquinas specifically states that the sensitive powers of apprehension do not receive virtue; in other words, the senses are not the subject of the virtues. They lead to knowledge, but at the level of sense perception there is not yet knowledge.

Student: It makes sense to say that the sensitive powers of apprehension are not the subject of virtue, since the senses tend to apprehend things as they are, and therefore sense perception and the way in which it occurs is not up to us, but depends on external factors.

Teacher: Exactly. In normal circumstances the senses perceive the external world as it is, and therefore their activity is not subject to moral improvement or otherwise.

4.1. The Unity of the Virtues

Student: Is it possible to have one virtue and not the others?

Teacher: This is a very important question, that of the unity of the virtues. Socrates discusses this problem in Plato's dialogue *Protagoras*, and it was also examined by Aristotle and Aquinas. It is possible to have one virtue and not the others, and to be good at some virtues rather than the others. However, perfect virtue means to have all the virtues.

Student: That would be the ideal virtuous person, perhaps the Stoic wise man?

Teacher: Yes, that is right, and later philosophers argued that Socrates, for instance, attained that ideal, in his life and in the way in which he accepted willingly to die for the truth and for justice. However, these ideals would be the exception rather than the rule. It can be argued that most people possess some virtues, and that some people possess more virtues than others, but complete virtue is very difficult to attain. However, that ideal remains the goal of those who strive in the path of virtue. That is why habit, particularly for philosophers in the Aristotelian tradition, is so important, as well as the search for knowledge. Intellectual and moral virtues must go hand in hand.

Student: Are there other aspects pertaining to the definition of virtue which we should take into account?

Teacher: The medieval philosophers, in particular the Scholastic philosophers, are very keen on analyzing everything from an Aristotelian perspective, by employing the terms of Aristotle's ten categories, which consist in substance and nine accidents. With regard to Plato, it is clear that he thought of virtue as a form, at least in the early dialogues, in which Socrates is looking for a definition of various virtues. In the dialogue *Meno*, he is searching for a universal definition of virtue which should in principle apply to everyone who is said to be virtuous (including children, women and slaves) and which does not change and is a permanent feature of those who are described as virtuous.

Student: The medieval philosophers must have a different account, since they were heavily influenced by Aristotle's logic and philosophy of language.

Teacher: That is right. Among the nine accidents that form part of Aristotle's ten categories (substance, quality, quantity, relation, place, time, position, possession, acting and being acted upon), several medieval philosophers identify virtue with quality, like Aureolus. Capreolus, for instance, thinks of it as a relation, rather than a form. For Aquinas, virtue is something that is absolute, but it is accompanied by a relation. Aureolus understands virtue as a quality which suits the nature in which it inheres, and it is something absolute which underlies a relation. Naturally, virtue is not a substance, since primary substances according to Aristotle are individual existing things.

However, virtue can be viewed as a quality that exists or resides in the soul. For Scotus, virtue is also a quality, but it can also be identified with a state, a habit and a disposition. For him, the virtues are situated in the higher faculties of human beings, and in that sense he does not accept Aquinas' understanding of the moral virtues as being in the irascible or concupiscible part of the soul. Scotus situates virtue in the higher faculties of the soul. Aquinas also thinks of virtue as something in between essence and operation, and also as a certain maximum of strength or power.

5. Types of Virtues

5.1. Moral and Theological Virtues

Student: We have concluded that virtue is something hard to attain.

Teacher: It is something that is up to us, and in our power, and it is in our nature to be able to develop virtue. However, it requires practice and a constant effort. Aristotle states that, regarding virtue or ethical action, there is only one way of getting it right, whereas there are many ways of getting ethical action wrong. Virtue is also a matter of precision, as we have mentioned.

Student: Is there a fixed number of virtues, or types for virtues?

Teacher: It is clear that Aristotle distinguishes two types of virtue, virtues of character, or moral virtues, and the intellectual virtues.

Student: What are the similarities and differences between them?

Teacher: One of the differences is that the virtues of thought are acquired through study and from teaching, or from a teacher, whereas the virtues of character are learned by practice, according to Aristotle.

Student: As you mentioned, it seems that the moral virtues stand for the typical virtues, such as justice and courage or temperance.

Teacher: Yes, but there is an important connection between moral and intellectual virtues, given that prudence is a central virtue, and it is considered to be an intellectual virtue, and closely connected with the moral virtues. Aquinas believes that the moral and the intellectual virtues need one another.

Student: If virtue is closely connected with reason then it makes sense to speak of the intellectual virtues as a separate type of virtue, and at the same time it is clear that prudence is closely connected with the moral virtues. The two types of virtue require one another.

Teacher: It does seem that the moral virtues represent the typical virtues, because of their association with ethics and morality. One could argue that these are the fundamental virtues since it is in principle not necessary to be knowledgeable in order to be virtuous, although that view might not be acceptable to all philosophers, as, for instance, Socrates.

Some translators and specialists, like Terence Irwin, prefer the term 'virtues of character', which is arguably broader or less specific than 'moral virtues' and appear to make way for other kinds of virtue. Equally, he refers to the 'virtues of thought' instead of the 'intellectual virtues'.

Student: Yes, it may be more customary to refer to the moral virtues and the intellectual virtues, but if we say virtues of character and virtues of thought they do not seem to be so different or far apart in the sense that a closer connection may be found between the two types of virtue.

Teacher: If we think of the moral virtues as the most representative ones, then that could be due to the possibility that the intellectual virtues might appear to be elitist, since they involve knowledge, which seems harder to attain. In turn, it might seem easier to attain the moral virtues, through practice. However, as we have seen, prudence is always required for moral action, as it appears to be involved in any kind of moral action.

Student: I understand that the moral virtues concern the way in which we deal with others or ourselves, whereas the virtues of thought pertain to the attainment of knowledge. Are there other differences between these two kinds of virtue?

Teacher: Yes, and there is a distinction between Plato and Aristotle in their approach to these two kinds of virtue. In Plato's dialogues, we encounter an analysis of various virtues, and in the early dialogues we find Socrates searching, with an interlocutor, for a suitable definition of certain virtues, like piety, friendship and courage, as we have seen. In the *Apology*, Socrates famously claims to be interested in human nature, rather than questions of astronomy or physics. Therefore, although virtue for him is about knowledge, it is about knowing how one should deal with others and live in society.

Student: It could be that the close link between virtue and knowledge may account for the fact that the Aristotelian distinction between moral and intellectual virtues is not clearly discernible in Plato's dialogues.

Teacher: I agree. In the *Republic*, Plato centers on the virtues which came be known as the four cardinal virtues, namely wisdom, courage, justice and temperance. However, they are to be found in the political state as a whole in this instance, as well as in the soul. The theory of the four cardinal virtues is later developed by Ambrose and is found also in Augustine and Aquinas, who explains why they are termed the cardinal virtues.

Student: Does the theory of the four cardinal virtues presuppose a clear distinction between virtues of character and virtues of thought?

Teacher: Perhaps so, because wisdom, termed prudence by Aquinas, is primarily a virtue of thought, whereas the other three are considered to be virtues of character. On the other hand, they are listed together by Plato and appear to form a unity. They are considered virtues of the state and also virtues of the different classes. In the *Republic*, courage is particularly associated with the class which defends the state, consisting as it does in facing dangers, whereas temperance consists in controlling the desires. Wisdom ('sophia') is particularly characteristic of the ruling class. Temperance is expected of everyone and it also brings the different classes together. The political state itself reproduces the structure of the human soul, and this constitutes another analogy between the virtues and the soul.

Student: Aristotle then makes a clearer distinction between the two types of virtue?

Teacher: That is correct, and he also does not have a theory of the four cardinal virtues. Rather he lists eleven virtues of character and five virtues of thought.

Student: If Aristotle makes a clear distinction between virtues of thought and virtues of character, he must think of their particular applications?

Teacher: The virtues of thought concern knowledge and Aristotle clearly thinks that the perfection of a human being must be based on a perfection of reason, hence the need for the theory of the intellectual virtues. Naturally, they must interact with the moral virtues, which consist in aligning the passions with reason, or curbing the passions. Reason always takes the lead, but the moral virtues imply an interaction between reason and the passions or the emotions.

Student: In what way do the moral virtues guide the passions?

Teacher: As we have seen, neither Aristotle nor Aquinas condemns the passions. There are different kinds of desire, but they are goal-directed, like the will or voluntary action. Unlike the Stoics later, Aristotle and Aquinas believe in the cooperation between reason and the passions or emotions.

Student: The Stoics believe that the passions always incline us to do evil, then?

Teacher: For the Stoics, the passions stand in opposition to reason, and they cloud reason. Among the passions, they distinguish mainly fear and wish or appetite, in other words, an attraction or repulsion towards their object. Cicero also applies these two principles to present and future events, adding hope and fear to describe emotions of attraction and repulsion concerning possible future events. The Stoics do not believe that the passions are natural, according to Cicero in the *Tusculan Disputations*. Cicero is a marvelous source on ancient and Hellenistic philosophy and he also provides his own distinct blend of philosophical ideas. And among the ancient schools of philosophy, he tends to side with either the Academicians, who were sceptics, or the Stoics.

Returning to the Stoics, simple impulses are not considered problematic, but the passions go beyond the measure of reason.

Student: The specific characteristic of the moral virtues is that they undertake a control of the passions, then?

Teacher: Yes, and the moral virtues bring the passions to a reasonable mean. Again, the moral virtues are not totally divorced from reason or intellect, since they must be guided by reason. Reason is the measure of virtuous action. As we have seen, virtuous action implies various elements, such as habit, which may not be in place initially but is certainly an important element of truly virtuous action. In addition, deliberation and decision decisively contribute to virtuous action. These operations imply the analysis of many aspects of the action to be carried out, in particular the circumstances. Therefore, it is clear that reason is strongly involved in morally virtuous action.

Student: Is there a difference between the use of reason within the framework of the moral virtues and in the intellectual virtues?

Teacher: As we have mentioned, the moral virtues are more closely associated with the active and the political life, in particular the virtue of justice, while the intellectual virtues go hand in hand with the contemplative life.

Student: And the cardinal virtues are developed by the medieval philosophers, particularly Aquinas?

Teacher: Aquinas is a very systematic writer, and in the *Summa Theologiae* he explains why they are termed the cardinal virtues, which is to say the fundamental or principal virtues. They concern the rectitude of appetite or will. The cardinal virtues concern the will and the attainment of good, and therefore they are the fundamental virtues. The intellectual virtues issue from the intellect.

Student: You mentioned another kind of virtue, the theological virtues.

Teacher: The theological virtues—faith, hope and charity—are formulated in a Christian context, based on Saint Paul's *First Epistle to the Corinthians*, and they are also developed by Aquinas. Naturally, they do not feature in Aristotle's text, or Plato's works. They are present in us in this life, but they pertain to a supernatural goal. Naturally, faith means faith in God, and particularly in God's existence as described in the Bible. Hope is tied to the expectancy of a future life after death. Charity means love towards God and others, but in light of God's love for us, so it has a supernatural character for us.

The theological virtues differ from the virtues devised by Aristotle, the moral and the intellectual virtues, in the sense that they do not originate in us; rather, they are infused by God. In addition, they are based on religious or sacred texts. We know of them from the Bible, in particular this epistle by Saint Paul. Whereas the other virtues are acquired by us through practice and by learning, the theological virtues are given to us by God.

Student: Some definitions of virtue, like the one provided by Augustine, which mentions that virtue is something that God produces in us, without us, imply that all virtue comes from God, do they not?

Teacher: During the medieval period, we find some definitions of virtue, for instance, the one provided by Augustine, which suggest that all virtue comes from God.

He means to say any predisposition to do good comes from God. Some scholars hold that Augustine thought of pagan virtue or ancient conceptions of virtue as a contradiction in terms, and that everything that was good in us came from God. However, in addition, Augustine also understands virtue more generally as the art of living rightly, and as the good use of free will.

Student: How does Aquinas receive Augustine's doctrine?

Teacher: Aquinas understands Augustine's doctrine, which is also adopted by Peter Lombard, in the light of Aristotelian ideas about virtue. We should not forget that in addition to his systematic works, in which virtue features prominently, such as the *Summa Theologiae*, and the *Summa contra Gentiles* (he also wrote the *Disputed Questions on Virtue*), he composed a detailed commentary on Aristotle's *Nicomachean Ethics*, in addition to other commentaries on Aristotle's works. This clearly shows a deep understanding of Aristotle's theory of virtue, and the effort that went into composing these commentaries bears testimony to Aquinas' interest in and respect for Aristotle's works and ideas.

Student: How does he reconcile a Biblical perspective on the virtues, and an appreciation for Augustine as a Patristic author, with Aristotle's views on virtue?

Teacher: He adopts Aristotle's understanding of the virtues as moral and intellectual, and adds the theological virtues, which he discusses in detail.

Student: The theological virtues are different from the moral and intellectual virtues in both nature and origin?

Teacher: That is correct. These virtues concern a supernatural object and end, God, and the goal of these virtues is the attainment of happiness in the hereafter.

Student: I understand that these virtues are infused in us by God, they are referred to in the Bible, specifically by Saint Paul in the New Testament, and their point of reference is God.

Are the theological virtues specifically Christian, and would this pose a problem to philosophers who are not Christian or have no religion?

Teacher: These are significant and important questions, which we should address after looking into the theological virtues in more detail. On the one hand, they appear to be specifically Christian. As we have seen, the origin of these virtues comes from the Biblical text, and therefore they have a Biblical origin. In addition, they refer to God, which again indicates a religious rather than a philosophical context. On the other hand, they have many points in common with the virtues which are studied by Aristotle and other ancient philosophers.

Student: If they have a strong religious connotation, does the term 'virtue' mean the same in the case of the theological and the other two kinds of virtue? Are there similarities between the theological virtues and Aristotle's conception of virtue?

Teacher: The theological virtues also admit of more or less. A person can have more charity than someone else. These virtues also imply an effort on the part of those who possess them. Although they are given by God, they require an effort on our part and they are of a practical nature. They constitute a certain power which can obtain certain good things for us and for others, and they have a voluntary element. The theological virtues clearly benefit those who have them and those who are in contact with those who have them. They also require habitual practice.

Student: As one of the theological virtues, must faith be given by God?

Teacher: Yes, faith comes from God, but human beings can exert an effort to receive that gift.

Student: We have seen that there are different kinds of virtue, and in particular the moral and the intellectual virtues, as devised by Aristotle. The theological virtues have a supernatural character in the sense that they are rooted in the love of God and their ultimate result is salvation in the next life. Does this mean that these virtues only have a meaning for Christians and for those who believe in the afterlife? Are they related to virtues or good qualities which are not religious?

Teacher: That is an interesting but complex point. On the one hand, those virtues are clearly rooted in the Christian tradition, as we have seen. Somehow, medieval Christian philosophers thought that the pagan virtues were not sufficient and in particular they did not suffice in the light of the prospect of salvation and our relationship with God. Moral and intellectual virtues were considered to be important from an ethical and political perspective, yet somehow the theological virtues, while helping us in this life, went beyond worldly considerations. If we look into the common aspects between the theological and the moral and intellectual virtues, charity, for instance, also means love towards others, and Saint Paul even states that this is the greatest of the three theological virtues. It resembles benevolence, a virtue which is highly esteemed by modern philosophers.

Faith and hope are related, respectively, to belief and trust, which are important in our daily dealings with others.

Student: Could we say that these virtues also have a philosophical and ethical meaning?

Teacher: Yes, they bear similarities to nonreligious virtues. Faith is closely linked to belief. Both faith and belief suggest an inner conviction and an acceptance of given facts or information without empirical proof or confirmation. Faith usually has religious connotations, since it means primarily, but not only, belief in God's existence, but even before the development of discussions about faith in Christianity there is philosophical literature on belief. For instance, in Plato's *Republic*, belief constitutes one of the elements of the divided line, ranking below reason or discursive reasoning and understanding or thought. These latter two belong to the domain of the intelligible, whereas belief, together with conjecture or imagination, belongs to the visible realm or the realm of the visible. Faith and belief tend to be associated with trust, and belief is also similar to opinion. There is justified belief, but exact confirmation eliminates any doubt and any uncertainty. For Socrates and Plato, belief can be something intermediate between ignorance and knowledge, but for the medieval philosophers and theologians, faith is a central virtue, in the sense that it is needed for salvation.

For the medieval philosophers and theologians, faith disappears in the next life, since that in which one has believed will be clearly seen. This interpretation of faith is also based on the New Testament, more specifically the *First Epistle to the Corinthians*.

Student: It seems that belief is broader than faith?

Teacher: Yes, faith is also belief, but belief does not always involve faith. Naturally, both faith and belief concern something theoretical, and in this sense they would be more aligned with the intellectual virtues than with the moral virtues. They both have a cognitive content and they play an essential role in our dealings with other people, since we regularly trust in the epistemic authority of other people. Trust can instead mean an attitude rather than a direct reference to the cognitive content of what is conveyed. Trust is vital because we cannot always verify the information that we receive. Indeed it seems that most of the information that we receive comes from other people rather than direct experience. Therefore faith, or belief, is essential both in our lives individually and in our dealings with other people.

Student: I understand how belief or faith is important in going about our daily lives.

Teacher: Yes, because we cannot always obtain certain knowledge, and belief is important by itself or as leading up to knowledge, when it becomes confirmed by evidence. Naturally, for the medieval philosophers, belief and faith acquire a new, richer meaning in the light of the authority of scripture, which invites us to assent to it.

Student: Yes, in the *Confessions*, Augustine remarks that we often accept people's authority on many issues. For instance, we learn from our parents about the date when we were born, and accept this information on their authority.

Teacher: Yes, belief and faith take on a whole new meaning in the works of Augustine. Believing in the scriptures becomes a virtue and it is actually meritorious to believe without proof or evidence. Faith becomes more important and valuable than knowledge.

Student: That makes sense, if we consider knowledge as part of the intellectual virtues and faith as a theological virtue. According to Christian philosophers and theologians, the theological virtues are more valuable or important than the other virtues, since they refer to God. Can we think of hope also in a nonreligious way?

Teacher: Hope is also related to trust, but its non-religious sense could be less obvious. In a religious context, hope implies primarily hope in the next life, in other words, hope in the survival of the soul and hope in the resurrection of the dead. For Aquinas, hope refers to the future, and some future good, and its object is something hard but possible to obtain. Hope can also be considered a passion, but as a theological virtue it must be situated in the higher faculties of the soul. In any case, hope points to some future happening and it consists in the expectation of something good. In this sense, hope is essential, for if we do not think that the future will bring some good, all motivation deserts us.

Student: Perhaps charity can also be understood in a nonreligious context?

Teacher: Yes, charity in a religious context means love, and in particular love of God, but also love of neighbor, as we have seen. It does not exclude love of oneself, since the Bible commands us to love God and our neighbor like ourselves.

Student: And this love can be transferred to others, by assisting them in some way.

Teacher: Yes, assisting others is a sign of our love for them. Love can have many meanings and perhaps for ancient Greek and Roman authors love expressed itself best as friendship, or by way of political alliances.

Student: It is certainly important to study friendship in detail, and also the similarities it bears to love.

Teacher: It is interesting to note that Aristotle, in the *Nicomachean Ethics*, devotes more attention to friendship than to any other virtue. He devotes Book 5 to justice, and Books 8 and 9 to friendship.

Student: How do we know that friendship is a kind of love?

Teacher: According to Aristotle, friendship also describes the relationship between parents and children, as well as between spouses, which indicates a broader conception of friendship than the one we have today. Other ancient authors, like Cicero, also think of friendship as a broad category and it always implies good will or benevolence. This kind of virtue, friendship or benevolence, is also highlighted by the British moralists.

Student: Friendship seems to build on the principle of altruism, which we have touched on earlier.

Teacher: Absolutely; we have commented on the debate between thinkers who hold that selfishness is the main driver of our actions and those who believe that we have altruistic motives. It seems that benevolence, which literally means wishing well with regard to others, is a central feature of friendship and also of virtue in general. Virtue seeks the good, as we have seen, and it seeks the good of others, while making us better.

Student: Is friendship a kind of disinterested love?

Teacher: That is right, true friendship is a disinterested bond. As we will see, there are different kinds of friendship, and not all of them have the other partner and his or her good as the end goal. Aristotle also mentions friendships where pleasure or utility is the main goal. However, the perfect kind of friendship implies practicing virtue towards others and wishing them well for their own sake. Cicero also thinks of complete virtue as this kind of perfect friendship.

Student: It seems that friendship highlights the most important aspects of virtue and its essential features?

Teacher: Certainly, because virtue implies doing good deeds and helping others, and friendship consists in just that. Therefore, we will devote more time to the discussion of friendship. It seems to be a special kind of benevolence, and essentially friendship derives from the benevolence we display towards others.

Student: Could one argue that we should love everyone and that friendship might consist in a selfish relationship with a few people to the detriment of others?

Teacher: In a sense, perhaps, but it would be very difficult to love everyone in the same way, especially people we do not know. In addition, we have special duties towards our relatives and close friends.

Student: That sounds right; it is more difficult to love and assist those who are further from us.

Teacher: Exactly, we must reach out first to those who are closest to us.

Student: Returning to the different types of virtues, we have seen that virtue can originate in us or come from God. However, according to Aquinas, not only the theological virtues are infused by God, correct?

Teacher: That is correct; the theological virtues are infused in us by God. However, Aquinas also mentions infused justice, for instance.

Student: In that case, it seems that all virtues are given by God. If that is so, one might argue that there would not be an active role for us in the acquisition of the virtues.

Teacher: For Aquinas, the infused moral virtues differ from the naturally acquired virtues in the sense that they direct us towards eternal life. In that way, they are not just oriented towards human ethical or political goals, but towards the facilitation of the attainment of salvation.

Student: I understand the difference between the naturally acquired moral virtues and the infused moral virtues. Perhaps we should concentrate on the moral and the intellectual virtues, since our focus is on virtuous action in this world, and towards others?

Teacher: That is perfectly fine. If we wish to follow primarily a philosophical rather than theological approach, then, we can delve into the moral and the intellectual virtues, since we have already explained the nature of the theological virtues, and the way in which they direct us towards the next life, according to the Christian tradition, and in particular according to Aquinas.

Student: Among the characteristics of virtue, we have seen that for Aristotle, virtue lies in a mean between extremes.

Teacher: That is a very important principle, and perhaps it is only by providing some examples that we can understand the golden mean concerning the virtues.

Student: Perhaps if we choose some of the virtues we can see how they consist in the mean.

Teacher: Yes. It also seems that the question of the mean bears on different aspects of the practice of the virtues. The passions have an important role to play when it comes to virtuous action, but we should not let ourselves be carried away by them. According to Aquinas in his *Commentary on the* Nicomachean Ethics, the mean should be observed in the virtues and also in the passions.

Student: Does it mean that the extremes which lie at either end of the virtues consist in excessive passion?

Teacher: Yes, that could be the case, or it could be the case of excessive passion at the higher end and lack of passion at the lower end of the spectrum.

Student: Perhaps we could discuss some particular virtues?

Teacher: After examining the elements that pertain to virtuous action, and the different types of virtue, Aristotle goes on to provide details on the specific virtues, to which we will now turn.

Student: We have seen that he specifically distinguishes the virtues of character and the virtues of thought.

Teacher: That is correct. Plato had not made this distinction, perhaps because for Socrates virtue always implies knowledge. When thinking of the ideal republic, Plato considers four main virtues, and one of them, wisdom or prudence, is considered a virtue of thought by Aristotle, while the other three, courage, justice and temperance, are considered to be virtues of character. In describing bravery or courage, Aristotle holds that it consists in the mean with regard to the feeling of fear and overconfidence.

Student: Courage means to control fear without being overconfident?

Teacher: Exactly. Aristotle understands fear as the expectation of some bad event, and courage has a role to play in dealing with frightening situations.

Student: According to that principle, courage means to conquer fear. On the one hand, it seems that the virtues imply the control of the emotions, as we have seen. In the case of courage, could it not be argued that it consists in doing away with fear altogether?

Teacher: The absence of fear does away with courage. Someone who has no fear, and consequently does not need to control it, is not said to be courageous but insensitive or perhaps overconfident. Courage means to conquer fear in certain situations, and also not to be overconfident. The situation must be judged, and the aim of courage, the virtue at stake in this case, is some good. One can be courageous in helping others, when it represents a risk to us. For instance, one could dip into a river in order to save someone who is being pulled by the current.

Student: Is it possible to say that the person is courageous even if the goal is not achieved?

Teacher: Yes. In principle, it is important to assess the circumstances, and ensure that one is strong enough to achieve the desired result — in this case, to save others from drowning. However, since the intention is central to ethical and virtuous action, it has a decisive role in judging whether an action is virtuous. Knowledge and deliberation are important, and assessing correctly the situation and the circumstances is also important, but in this case the courageous or brave act is based primarily on the strength of the intention to do good. Assessment of the situation implies the calculation of risks, for it might be difficult, in this case, to judge the strength of the current without plunging into it.

Student: And courage also implies controlling our fear of certain things that we naturally avoid, like pain and death, or any kind of suffering.

Teacher: Yes, that is the kind of situation which we fear, and those are the main objects of fear, and which require courage, particularly in extreme situations. Aristotle states that we can fear many things, like the loss of reputation, but courage applies to fear of specific situations. He considers courage in the face of death, in a war situation, as the height of courage, presumably if one is fighting for one's country and for a good cause.

Student: And the lack of courage would be cowardice?

Teacher: Yes, in situations in which it would be expected that one should help.

Student: Does courage apply to actions or also to words?

Teacher: One could be courageous in telling the truth, when it is called for, absolutely.

Student: And does courage always imply helping others, or one's country or community?

Teacher: We can also consider situations when courage reflects on the agent of the brave action. One can endure pain, for instance, when seeking a higher goal such as winning a sports competition, or making a particular effort that goes towards one's improvement while involving pain.

Student: Perhaps the notion of sacrifice is also an act of courage?

Teacher: Yes, it can be, if it means giving up something that is part of our physical or mental well-being.

Student: Perhaps not everyone fears the same things?

Teacher: That is right. Aristotle, who in the *Nicomachean Ethics* discusses courage as the first of the moral virtues, states that different people may fear different things.

Student: Is it actually possible not to be afraid?

Teacher: Apparently, some people lack a sense of fear, although according to current medical research this is a very rare condition. In that case, as we have mentioned, one is arguably not courageous. And perhaps these people are also not reckless, but lack a cognitive or sensitive function. This would be a very rare phenomenon. Naturally, fear is extremely important in keeping us alive and well, especially when we are faced with difficult situations and need to find a way of preserving our well-being.

Student: Does Aristotle apply his general criterion of virtue to courage?

Teacher: Yes, he states in the *Nicomachean Ethics* that courage implies fearing the right things and facing them in the right way, and at the right time, for the right end.

Student: Does that mean that we should not help people who do not deserve it or who are not good?

Teacher: Well, perhaps it is better to help first those who need it most and those who are good. However, Christian doctrine definitely implies helping everyone, including enemies, or at least praying for them, and generally doing something good for them. That would also constitute an act of courage.

Student: Would Aristotle have a different approach?

Teacher: In general, one can think of different degrees of courage, and Aristotle considers circumstances as an important part of virtue. Because in his kind of society women were not likely to participate in wars, they would have fewer opportunities to show their courage or bravery.

Student: But if facing pain and distress are part of what makes one courageous, then they would have many opportunities to display courage.

Teacher: Yes, they would. But naturally, it is important to think of Aristotle's words not just in general but also within the context in which he was formulating his theories. Indeed he argues that customs change from place to place, and also what is considered to be virtuous. In that way, his views are very different from those of Plato and Socrates.

Student: The Stoics would have a different view on courage, would they not? They would argue that complete disregard of pain, and thus perhaps a certain kind of insensitivity, would constitute perfect courage, and generally speaking not only disregard for death but also pain?

Teacher: Yes, in the *Tusculan Disputations*, Cicero, who did not follow a particular school, but chose his position according to the theory in question, discusses the possibility of someone being happy while they are being tortured. This would constitute perfect virtue and would be an example of the perfectly virtuous person.

Student: We have seen that the Stoic wise man is a very rare person.

Teacher: Let us return to our description of courage as provided by Aristotle. He also says that the courageous person is hopeful, unlike a coward, who loses hope.

Student: We have seen how hope need not only be a theological virtue but can be a secular or nonreligious virtue, in the sense that it leads us to expect that things will turn out well and fellow human beings will take the right course of action. However, it is possible that Aristotle is thinking here of hope as an affection rather than a virtue, as opposed to fear.

Teacher: That is right, and later the Stoics would focus on four main kinds of emotions, which Cicero describes in his works, in particular the *Tusculan Disputations*, as we have seen. According to him, the emotions are based on belief. More specifically, they concern belief in what is good or bad, regarding present or future affairs. Delight ('laetitia') is belief that some good is present while longing ('libido') is the expectation of something good in the future. Distress ('aegritudo') concerns belief in something bad currently happening while fear ('metus') pertains to the expectation of some evil that is to come. If we think of hope as the expectation of some good to come, then perhaps hope can also be an emotion. In this sense, if hope means too much confidence, then it becomes an obstacle to true courage.

Student: Since some contemporary authors have argued that it can be a virtue, how do we know whether hope is a virtue or an emotion?

Teacher: Both virtues and the emotions imply a cognitive element. Emotions involve a certain kind of belief, in particular a belief regarding whether something good or bad is going to affect us, and also whether it is something good or bad in itself. In that sense, emotions are not some irrational response. Through the emotions, we can have an intuitive response that is only later formulated at the rational level. In that sense, the emotions can perceive and understand something more quickly than our rational part.

Student: And virtuous action also presupposes knowledge.

Teacher: That is correct, as we have seen, since it always implies an assessment of the situation. However, the virtues are more explicitly or clearly linked to reason and the exercise of our intellectual and mental abilities. Emotions are more immediate reactions, even if they involve knowledge or belief, while virtue requires a special effort and in particular a greater intellectual effort. The virtues can be acquired by habit and the emotions can be educated, but they are different. Virtue, as we have seen, involves the emotions for most philosophers, even if the Stoics are not part of that majority.

Student: Also, it seems that the emotions do not necessarily produce the same as the virtues, by way of good effects.

Teacher: I agree, the emotions can lead to some good deed, but it is virtue that truly constitutes a power, more than the emotions. In fact, virtue consists in the control and harnessing of the emotions in order to practice a good deed.

According to Aristotle, both excessive confidence and excessive fear lead to lack of courage, and more generally both excess and defect detract from virtue.

Student: Then courage is also a matter of a certain precision?

Teacher: Yes, it has to be the right mean between rashness and cowardice, and that may be difficult to attain. Aristotle states that courage is particularly obvious in the most frightening situations, such as a situation of war, but there are many other situations which we can think of as opportunities to exercise courage. Accepting certain duties may be a sign of courage, or facing a situation that requires doing the right thing and that can challenge our health or well-being. In detailing the situations in which courage is experienced, Aristotle mentions political contexts, requiring that one defend one's country or people. The same goes for virtue in general and courage, in the sense that courage must issue from us and not constitute an action carried out by compulsion.

In commenting on Socrates' conception of virtues (probably Aristotle is referring to Plato's dialogue *Protagoras*), Aristotle agrees that knowledge tends to add to courage. In that dialogue, Socrates challenges the view that courage has anything to do with impetuousness, and that in fact knowledge indicates greater confidence. For him, courage does not come from being physically stronger, which makes sense, since Socrates holds that virtue resides in the soul.

Student: Aristotle also holds that courage as a virtue becomes part of one's character, as an enduring character trait?

Teacher: That is correct, and in that sense, one is able to react courageously in a situation when one does not have advance warning. Courage becomes like second nature. If one is caught off guard, one can still react in a courageous way. Virtue becomes like an ingrained habit and not just a matter of reflection and calculation, which require more time. Obviously, that is a great difference with regard to Socrates' position.

Student: You also mentioned that virtue is something hard to attain.

Teacher: It is, and that also applies to courage, since it means reacting so as to conquer fear and face something that could be painful. Aristotle states that it is easier to abstain from something pleasant than to face something painful. He gives the example of physical exercise and one's participation in athletic contests.

Student: Courage is later considered one of the cardinal virtues, but for Aristotle it is one of several virtues of character, correct?

Teacher: Yes, and in the *Nicomachean Ethics*, Aristotle proceeds to the treatment of temperance, another essential virtue according to Cicero, and already mentioned by Plato as one of the four main virtues.

Student: Temperance is something akin to self-control?

Teacher: That is correct, and it also plays a very important role in Plato's dialogues, especially with regard to the body and the curbing of its excessive demands. Aristotle describes it after courage because he holds, as Aquinas would do later, that both courage and temperance involve a control of nonrational parts of the soul that can obey the intellect. Aquinas states that courage and temperance concern the irascible and the concupiscible parts of the soul, respectively.

Student: And for Aristotle temperance also concerns the mean between two extremes.

Teacher: Yes, it consists in the mean with regard to pleasures. Here Aristotle makes a distinction between pleasures of the soul and pleasures of the body. This had already been the topic of discussion in Plato's *Philebus*. For Aristotle love of learning and love of honor are among the pleasures of the soul, since they do not affect the body but the soul.

Student: These seem to be good pleasures, which do not affect us in a negative way?

Teacher: Absolutely, and in that sense Aristotle states that these pleasures do not concern the virtue of temperance. Honor is a good thing, as well as learning, and therefore a mean is not to be searched for in this case. With regard to other pleasures of the soul, which can be distracting, like storytelling, temperance or intemperance is not an issue.

Student: In that case, temperance concerns the pleasures of the body.

Teacher: Yes, and specific pleasures of the body. When we think of bodily pleasure, we think of sensation and in particular the five senses, and the way they are affected. They can be affected in several ways, including pleasurable and painful ways.

Student: And Aristotle has certain specific senses in mind?

Teacher: Exactly. Pleasures of sight or hearing do not count among the pleasures that need to be controlled, according to Aristotle. For him, listening to music or seeing paintings are not activities that come under the umbrella of temperate or intemperate actions. Smell also does not seem to relate to temperance. Therefore temperance has to do with the enjoyment or consumption of things, like eating and drinking.

Student: Eating and drinking clearly have a precise measure. One should not drink or eat too much.

Teacher: I agree, and with regard to drinking the concern seems to be primarily with intoxicating drinks, although it is even possible to drink too much water, or other kinds of liquids.

Student: It appears that eating and drinking in moderation would simply require good sense, so why is the control of this kind of consumption considered to be a virtue?

Teacher: In the case of these excesses, perhaps we are not hurting others when eating too much, or too little, at least not directly, but we would be hurting ourselves. And in order to be virtuous, we should not practice any kind of excess in our habits. Virtue is about the excellence of human character and nature, and these kinds of excesses do not belong in that framework.

Student: If temperance does not concern seeing, hearing or smelling, then it must concern touch and taste.

Teacher: Yes, but it is really essentially about touch, and the quantities involved. Taste consists in distinguishing flavors, but intemperance in this case is when one drinks or eats too much, and Aristotle believes that this has more to do with touch than taste.

Student: And again, it is a matter of excess?

Teacher: Exactly. Eating and drinking are normal activities, indeed they are necessary, but there is the right measure for them. There may be differences of taste, but it is important to avoid excesses. It is also important to avoid the wrong kind of food.

Student: Aristotle would probably have included many current types of food among those that are to be avoided.

Teacher: Probably, if they are not nutritious and are harmful to our health.

Student: In that case, temperance is about avoiding certain pleasures and courage is about withstanding certain pains.

Teacher: Precisely. And the intemperate person is the one who follows these kinds of pleasures and makes them his or her priority.

Student: In this case, is the mean always the best option? I am thinking of traditions, in several religions, of fasting and refraining from marriage.

Teacher: Yes. In the case of fasting, it is done for specific purposes, and should not harm one's health, which means that even in fasting there should be moderation.

In comparison with marriage and the need for reproduction, this is something that Aquinas mentions in the *Summa Theologiae*. There is a fundamental distinction between eating and drinking on the one hand, and reproduction, on the other. Eating and drinking concern the individual, in particular the survival of the individual, and therefore they cannot be given up. However, activities related with reproduction concern the survival of the species, and therefore they can be entirely given up by some individuals, for religious reasons, for instance.

Student: We have seen that for later Aristotelians virtue is not always the question of the golden mean.

Teacher: Yes, and for instance when it comes to the theological virtues, it is not clear that there is a mean, in the sense that the more hope, faith and charity, the better. Aristotle also thinks of temperance as a mean, because someone who is insensible to these pleasures, he believes, is not really human. There are also right and wrong types of pleasures, but the question of the mean is central.

Student: Would not the Stoics take a different position later?

Teacher: Yes, and although the Stoics did not think that physical pleasure or external goods contributed to happiness, they considered them as indifferents and held that they could constitute a certain kind of good, albeit not an essential one. Aristotle himself holds that the temperate person does not find intense pleasure in bodily things and is not concerned by their absence. Instead, he or she will enjoy the things that lead to health and fitness, and obviously enjoy them in the right way and at the right time, in accordance with reason.

Student: Intemperance would be the opposite type of attitude with regard to these pleasures?

Teacher: Yes. Aristotle also holds that intemperance has a more voluntary character, in the sense that it is easier to exercise self-control than to practice courage—he had already said that it was easier to refrain from pleasure than to withstand pain.

Student: It seems that it is easier to be temperate than to be courageous.

Teacher: Yes, and in particular circumstances, it seems that the voluntary element can be limited, if someone, for instance, in a situation of war, avoids pain by refraining from fighting. It could be argued that it is easier to acquire the habit of temperance than to become accustomed to be brave. Probably the occasions for being temperate are more easily recognized and predicted, whereas the occasions for courage are more difficult to foresee and involve more fundamental decisions regarding our well-being and that of those around us. Aristotle adds that cowardice seems to be more voluntary at the general level, and intemperance at the level of particular actions. Aristotle states that no one wants to be intemperate.

Student: Temperance is also a question of acquiring good habits?

Teacher: Yes, and Aristotle associates some of the errors of children with a certain tendency towards intemperateness, hence the need for training and habituating them to acquire temperate habits. In general, there is a need to follow reason, as is the case with the other virtues.

Student: Aristotle also thinks of generosity as a virtue.

Teacher: Yes, for Aristotle generosity is the mean in questions of wealth, especially in the matter of giving. In this case, it is important not to keep too much for ourselves, which would lead to ungenerosity, nor to give too much in a wasteful way, so as to become ruined. Wealth is a means to an end and not the goal. It is the kind of good which is useful, and therefore it constitutes a means to an end and not the end itself. Here Aristotle takes the opportunity to state that virtue is more about doing good than receiving it.

Student: This would amount to helping others?

Teacher: Yes, and in the case of generosity, he states that it is easier not to take than to give, and therefore giving requires more effort and is more virtuous. Virtue is also about being good, an element that underlies all the virtues. However, it is more important to give than to take, naturally. Aristotle, for whom assessing the circumstances is always essential, also states that it is important to give in the right way, at the right time, to the right people, in the right amount. Generosity also entails giving with pleasure, and this is perhaps clearer than in the other virtues previously discussed, courage and temperance.

In addition, wealth must come from the right source, and in giving one should pay attention to others, not to oneself. Aristotle considers more important the quality than the quantity of what is given, and the state of the giver with regard to the proportion of what we give in relation to what we have. One may give less and be more generous, if the amount is greater in proportion to one's possessions.

Student: If giving reduces one's wealth, could that become a problem?

Teacher: That is a characteristic of the generous person, and it becomes a paradox, because the virtuous, who deserve to be wealthier, become less wealthy. However, their primary goodness does not consist in material goods, but in being virtuous. Equally, in giving one should not exceed one's means.

Student: Yes, I am certain that it would not be considered generous to borrow in order to give, or to steal in order to give.

Teacher: Precisely, that would not constitute a virtue but instead a vice. Generosity is the mean between giving and taking, according to Aristotle, and it also consists in spending on the right projects, while taking pleasure in giving.

Student: Would seeking wealth in order to give constitute generosity?

Teacher: If the funds are received in the right way, then that is fine. Receiving in the right way, in this case, also pertains to generosity. The generous person is easy and pleasant to work with in financial matters.

Student: Clearly, for Aristotle, money is a means to an end, and not the end.

Teacher: Money can and should be the opportunity to do good and to help others, more than helping ourselves.

Student: What are the extremes to avoid in relation to generosity?

Teacher: Spending too much or in the wrong way is wastefulness, and not spending enough is lack of generosity.

Student: I wonder if these extremes are equally bad?

Teacher: Aristotle holds that the lack of generosity is worse in this case, because the wasteful person can learn to become moderate in time.

Student: Maybe the difference between wastefulness and lack of generosity, in this sense, has to do with the way one donates in addition to the recipient of the donation?

Teacher: Yes, all that should also be taken into consideration. Giving to the wrong people can have disastrous consequences. However, Aristotle appears to think that lack of generosity is more difficult to correct, and is a stronger tendency in human beings, that is to say, the tendency not to give. Also, there seem to be more ways of being ungenerous than of being wasteful according to Aristotle, for it includes not only giving too little, or not giving at all, but also taking too much, although some people who do not give also do not take or do not take too much.

Student: Generosity too seems to imply a fine balance.

Teacher: Yes, and again, being generous should be done in a fairly precise way, but one can be wasteful and ungenerous in several ways and for different reasons.

Student: One could perhaps argue that in the same way that there is a unity of virtues, there is also unity of vices?

Teacher: That is possible; in the same way that the virtuous person will have several virtues, the vicious person will display several vices, and one vice is often accompanied by others. In the case of the excesses pertaining to generosity, stealing from a temple, for instance, means impiety more than ungenerosity. Loving gain beyond measure is also an excess with respect to generosity. Gambling and stealing are vices that come under the rubric relating to generosity.

Student: Aristotle's assessment of generosity remains extremely pertinent.

Teacher: Yes, generosity is still extremely important and a very important way to help others and share our goods. One could give to friends, family, charity and anyone who needs financial help, or people and institutions for which financial help will make a difference.

Student: Where else does Aristotle observe a greater tendency towards ungenerosity than wastefulness in human nature?

Teacher: The ungenerous include those who gamble and steal, for they are taking funds that are most needed. Aristotle analyzes human nature in broad strokes and in particular cases when it comes to the question of virtue, offering descriptions of the different virtues.

Student: In the *Nicomachean Ethics*, Aristotle goes on to analyze other virtues.

Teacher: Yes, he mentions other moral virtues, and some of them have an important place in ancient Greek society, and seem to relate to Aristotle's own views on politics and the connection between ethics and politics.

Student: We have seen that this is a central connection for Aristotle, but would it be possible in principle to separate virtue from politics—in other words, to have virtue regardless of politics, or perhaps politics without virtue?

Teacher: For those philosophers who find fault with virtue ethics, perhaps the law could replace the virtues, but even so, the laws are not so specific that they can guide action in each case and instance. Naturally, the common good underlies the laws and national constitutions, in order to allow society to flourish and prosper, but virtue would still be needed. On the other hand, virtue naturally leads to politics in the sense that it cannot be practiced in isolation and that it should find support within a political framework.

Student: We could also think of common or social virtues as opposed to individual ones?

Teacher: Exactly. Generosity, for instance, can be conceived as the generosity of the state, which could include the lack of corruption which can be generated by wastefulness.

Student: One could argue that Aristotle views virtue primarily as the duty of the individual, whereas it could have greater effect if embedded in societal structures.

Teacher: Yes, some scholars might argue in that direction. However, we saw that in the *Republic*, Plato associates certain virtues with certain classes, which indicates a communal understanding of virtue. In addition, justice seems to underlie the other virtues too, in the sense of constituting the right measure in dealing with others.

Student: Can virtue be generally sought and found at the societal level?

Teacher: That certainly seems to be something highly desirable. Returning to your question about the link between politics and virtue, it would appear that politics requires virtue at the level of the individuals and at the level of political structures. In other words, we expect politicians to be virtuous and even role models, and to sacrifice personal benefit to the common good. On the other hand, it would in principle be possible to practice virtue at the individual level, towards one or a few individuals, or a few individuals at a time, but since we are political animals, as Aristotle states, the political dimension soon comes into play, and one must think not only at the individual level but also at the level of society.

Student: In connection with generosity, does Aristotle describe other virtues?

Teacher: Yes, another virtue, similar to generosity, is magnificence, but this term signifies the expenditure of large amounts rather than generosity, broadly speaking. In any case, the money would have to be well spent.

Student: This virtue can only be practiced by someone who is very wealthy.

Teacher: That is correct. We can think of examples of philanthropy in our day and age. The extremes of this virtue lie in stinginess, if too little is spent, or poor taste if too much is spent but in the wrong way, and in order to show off. As with the other virtues, the magnificent person aims at what is fine or beautiful and good.

Student: Magnificence is generosity on a grand scale, then.

Teacher: That is right, and according to Aristotle, this includes spending on religious works or public works for the city. Naturally, this virtue is for a minority of people, but those who are wealthy are expected to have it.

He also mentions magnanimity, which is the virtue concerning great things, and this also seems to be for a minority of people.

Student: I wonder what kind of great things Aristotle means in the case of magnanimity?

Teacher: For instance, the kind of things that will lead to honor, which as stated by Aristotle is the greatest of the external goods.

Student: Honor concerns what people think of us?

Teacher: Yes, and one might wonder why this is important or something that pertains to virtue. Aristotle states that the magnanimous person is good and worthy of the best things.

Student: But in the case of this virtue, one also has to have the right opinion of oneself, with respect to goodness?

Teacher: Yes, one should only think oneself worthy of great things if one is truly good and able to do those great things.

Student: If honor is about what people think of us, then how does it have to do with our own actions?

Teacher: Presumably, one attains honor in society if one distinguishes oneself for particular deeds or feats. For Aristotle, this virtue crowns the other virtues and it is tied to honor on account of good deeds. This virtue can be practiced only by a minority of people but it does not necessarily require wealth. It can result from doing great things in battle or in politics, and it is possible that Aristotle has the Homeric heroes in mind. This virtue concerns honor and Aristotle states that the gods are the worthiest of honor.

Student: This does not mean seeking fame, but it indicates a concern for honor?

Teacher: In the case of magnanimity, one has to be famous or receive honors and recognition for the right reasons, that is to say, for being truly good and doing great things, and not just for accidental traits, or for moving in the right kind of society. Fame or honor is a result of being truly virtuous and therefore this virtue is the crown of the other virtues.

Student: Surely the question of honor and fame is discussed by other philosophers?

Teacher: Yes. For instance, for Cicero it is important to be virtuous in general and to distinguish oneself in politics, but fame is not something that one can truly control. It is important to do good things and it is good if these are recognized by others. However, we cannot really control the way people think about us, and so this should not be our priority. Aquinas, too, in the *Summa contra Gentiles*, states that we should not base our happiness on what others think of us, since this is not within our control. This means that for him happiness does not consist in honor, but it is good to be worthy of honor.

Student: Sometimes our good deeds are not known, and it is also possible for someone to have a bad reputation in spite of doing good deeds.

Teacher: Exactly, and therefore Cicero and Aquinas do not rate this kind of good as highly as Aristotle. However, Aristotle states that magnanimity must be based on true goodness and it cannot consist in a reputation for something that we did not do. The magnanimous person also has to have the other virtues and be generally good.

Student: In that sense, the goal would not be honor itself, but honor would be sought as a result of being good?

Teacher: Precisely. Honor would not be something truly essential in comparison with virtue and being good, but it would be a recognition of true virtue and being good in general. Magnanimity also means being great in each virtue.

Student: Could magnanimity represent the possession and overlapping of the various virtues?

Teacher: That is right. We have seen that the unity of the virtues is a recurrent theme among ancient and medieval philosophers, and the link between the virtues is also very important. Several philosophers state that possessing one virtue often means possessing the others, or some of the other virtues. They also state that wisdom or prudence is necessary for any action involving the moral virtues. Accordingly, Aristotle states that the magnanimous person must also be courageous and just, otherwise that person's actions would be shameful. According to Aristotle, magnanimity adorns the other virtues and completes them. In addition, the magnanimous person is not unduly concerned with power and wealth, or good or ill fortune.

Student: The opposite of magnanimity would perhaps be shame?

Teacher: Shame is also considered to be a virtue, so according to Aristotle magnanimity and shame are connected as virtues, as we will see.

Student: Regarding magnanimity, surely material possessions are not the most important factor for the magnanimous person?

Teacher: No, being good is the most important factor, even if the right circumstances and material possessions can maximize one's good actions and behavior. In addition, Aristotle holds that magnanimity is related to honor, but it has to be based on goodness.

Student: Would you say that the question of having a good name is more important in ancient Greece or Rome, than, for instance, in medieval Europe?

Teacher: Yes, but Cicero, in the Dream of Scipio, a text which is part of book 6 of his *De Republica*, has Scipio belittling fame, stating that our names will not be remembered for long, and stressing the importance of virtue. In the Middle Ages, naturally, under Christian influence, the most important kind of fame is what God, rather than human beings, thinks about us.

Student: It also seems that, when it comes to spending in a virtuous way, the mean varies from person to person or from virtue to virtue?

Teacher: Exactly. Aristotle states that magnificence exceeds generosity in the amount that is spent. It is clear that magnanimity can also imply a large spending, although it is not primarily about giving or spending. Magnanimity pertains to great causes and to doing good more than receiving it. Accordingly, the magnanimous think more of what they give than what they receive.

Student: Does the magnanimous person seek to be superior to other people?

Teacher: Yes, although competition in this sense might be something good if it promotes virtuous action. In addition, the magnanimous person speaks the truth and is generally not afraid of speaking her mind. Aristotle also emphasizes the self-sufficiency of this person. Curiously, the magnanimous person is not keen on productive possessions, since they are the means to an end rather than the end itself.

Student: What would be the extremes in the case of this virtue?

Teacher: The extremes would be the pusillanimous person, someone who is too humble, on the one hand, and the person who is excessive in seeking honor, when they are not worthy of it, on the other.

Student: There is also a virtue concerned with small honors, is there not?

Teacher: That is correct. Aristotle states that magnificence relates to generosity in the way it requires higher spending, and magnanimity relates to the virtue which is concerned with smaller honors, which does not have a specific name. It pertains to desiring honor in the right way, from the right sources and in the right measure. It concerns seeking honor in the right way.

Student: This nameless virtue would be more easily practiced than magnanimity, then?

Teacher: Yes, and it means that seeking honor according to our status is important.

Student: Is there a particular political significance to this virtue, if one is honored for helping one's community?

Teacher: That would be a valid inference.

Student: Aristotle mentions other virtues as part of the moral virtues, does he not?

Teacher: Aristotle goes on to describe mildness as the virtue which concerns the mean with regard to anger.

Student: This means that Aristotle does not consider a complete absence of anger to be a good or a virtuous thing.

Teacher: Precisely. He does not have a name for the extremes in the case of this virtue, but they clearly constitute a lack of anger or excessive anger. And excess is a kind of irascibility. The right amount of anger is when someone is angry at the right people, at the right time, in the right way. In this case, however, the tendency towards deficiency is preferable.

Student: Complete lack of anger is also blameworthy.

Teacher: Exactly, and this consists, for example, in accepting insults to oneself or one's friends without a response.

Student: Could there be a connection between moderate anger and justice?

Teacher: Yes, and the virtues often go together, as we have seen. When it comes to excessive anger, Aristotle mentions those who get very angry, and those who stay angry for a long time, the choleric and the bitter people, respectively. Irascible people do not stay angry for a long time. Irritable people also belong in the category of those who are angrier than is proper. Aristotle states that the tendency is for us to be angry rather than to incline to the other extreme. It is more common to wish for a penalty for the offender than to disregard the offense. Aristotle adds that it is difficult to establish the exact circumstances in which one should be angry, namely, the people against whom one should be angry, as well as the motive and the manner of being angry.

Student: There should always be fairness in the way we deal with others, then?

Teacher: Absolutely, and already Plato thought of justice as a kind of overarching virtue that is involved in every virtuous action.
Aristotle also mentions the virtue of friendliness.

Student: In what way is friendliness different from friendship?

Teacher: Friendliness is a distinct virtue, and it consists in being pleasant in our dealings with one another. It is similar to friendship, but does not seem to be directed at particular people who are our friends, but to be pleasant to everyone around us, whether they are close to us or not. In addition, it does not require a special feeling. It involves treating people in the right way.

Student: Does it involve treating everyone in the same way?

Teacher: Not exactly in the same way, according to Aristotle. People who are considered particularly worthy are treated differently by the friendly person, as well as people he or she knows more intimately.

Student: In that case, then, there would not be equality in our treatment of others.

Teacher: The friendly person would be friendly in the right way according to the circumstances and particularly according to the object of friendliness, the people to whom one is friendly. Aristotle also states that this person will avoid causing pain or sharing particular pleasures, so that this does not constitute particular friendship. In addition, being friendly also means to have no ulterior motive for one's action; otherwise this is called flattery.

Student: I understand that this is a virtue which is connected with sociability. One should generally be pleasant to others in social dealings, while taking account of specific circumstances.

What would be the opposites?

Teacher: The flatterer would exaggerate and wish to obtain something out of being friendly, while the quarrelsome person would likely cause pain.

Aristotle also thinks of truthfulness as a virtue and one that pertains to social interactions and to what one says about oneself, in particular what the virtuous person says about him- or herself.

For Aquinas, in the *Summa Theologica*, friendliness and truthfulness are parts of justice, and he brings several Aristotelian virtues under the umbrella of the cardinal virtues, while identifying other virtues as belonging to the cardinal virtues, such as religion and piety, which are parts of justice. For him magnificence is a part of courage, as well as patience and perseverance, which are virtues in their own right. In devising new moral virtues and associating them with the cardinal virtues the influence of Cicero is patent. Aquinas follows Cicero in stating that continence, mildness and modesty are parts of temperance. Aquinas also thinks of clemency, meekness, humility and studiousness as parts of temperance.

Student: I understand. For Aristotle, truthfulness is a mean between which extremes?

Teacher: It is a mean between boastfulness and self-deprecation about one's own deeds, and it has no ulterior motive than to tell the truth about oneself.

Student: Could this be a virtue that included telling the truth in general?

Teacher: That might be more related to the intellectual virtues, but telling the truth is certainly an absolute principle for some philosophers, such as Kant. Aristotle states that telling the truth in matters of justice concerns a different virtue. According to Aristotle, it may be appropriate to be reserved about one's good deeds, so it is more important to avoid excess than deficiency in this virtue. Consequently, boastfulness is further from telling the truth than being humble about one's deeds, and therefore boastfulness is especially to be avoided.

Student: Being truthful about oneself also seems to be important for the magnanimous person, as we have seen.

Teacher: That is right, and again we see how having some virtues requires having or practicing other virtues.

Teacher: Aristotle also mentions wit as a virtue, correct?

Teacher: Yes, it should be exercised in an informal context in meeting people and saying the right things. One should not speak too much or too little, or disregard the kind of audience one is speaking to. Like friendliness, it seems to imply a specific social skill.

Student: Aristotle thinks that relaxation is important and, in this context, being witty is very important.

Teacher: Exactly, and naturally in ancient Greece there were formal social meetings and informal social meetings. Examples of the former could be political meetings, and an example of the latter could be the kind of meeting described in Plato's *Symposium*, like an informal dinner. Wit, as well as friendliness and truthfulness, concerns general dealings with people, and truthfulness concern the truth, while wit and friendliness concern the pleasurable.

Aristotle also mentions shame, while noting that it is more a feeling than a virtue, or state of character. It is a kind of fear, particularly of falling into disrepute. He says that feeling shame is more appropriate of young people. One should be ashamed of base actions, which means that the virtuous person would not find the occasion to feel shame, or would not give rise to that occasion. Aristotle also mentions decency and justice to oneself, but since they follow from justice, we should analyze justice first.

Student: Justice was also a very important virtue for Plato, as we have seen. And if we think of it as giving others their due, then it seems that justice could be the main moral virtue and in a certain way it would appear to be present in all the other moral virtues. We could think of giving others their due in terms of what they deserve by way of material and spiritual goods.

Teacher: I agree, and for Plato justice was certainly a central virtue, in various dialogues, but particularly in the *Republic*. It is the subject of Book I of the *Republic*, and it also features in the other books of the *Republic*. It is a multifaceted virtue in the sense that it includes interpersonal relations but it also has a strong political aspect in its role of structuring the political community.

Student: How does Aristotle view justice?

Teacher: He thinks it is complete virtue given that it implies treating others in the right way. Justice is the good of another person, since justice to ourselves comes under a different rubric. In this context, Aristotle also says that the ruler's virtue or otherwise is immediately recognized or thrown into focus, because the ruler necessarily deals with the problems of others.

Student: Even today we find that political leaders are under close scrutiny, and every action is examined.

Teacher: Aristotle says that justice is another person's good because it benefits others rather than ourselves.

Student: Perhaps it is the virtue that most clearly shows that aspect of virtue, since other virtues also benefit others. Does not courage benefit others?

Teacher: Yes, and perhaps temperance is the virtue that most clearly benefits the subject of the action, while justice is the virtue that most clearly benefits others since it is directly aimed at others. Aristotle also seems to have in mind the exchange of goods as a central object of this virtue, like wealth but also honor. In this sense justice is complete virtue, and includes the laws, but it should also govern personal relationships.

Student: Aristotle accepts that there is more than one type of justice?

Teacher: Yes, he argues that this is a communal virtue as well as an interpersonal virtue.

Student: Perhaps that is why it is such an important virtue for Aristotle, since it possesses that communal or political dimension, in addition to the individual dimension?

Teacher: Yes, and Aristotle devotes more attention to justice than to the other moral virtues, if we exclude friendship, since book 5 of the *Nicomachean Ethics* is devoted to justice and to the various kinds of justice. He devotes even more attention to friendship, as we shall see.

Student: How does he view justice in a special sense?

Teacher: Justice in a special sense pertains to fairness and equal giving, in other words, equality in relation to the people involved and to the goods distributed. Aristotle argues that different political systems value different goods: namely, in democracy free citizenship is prized above all else, while oligarchy focuses on wealth, and champions of aristocracy defend the principle that virtue is the highest good. Justice is also about proportionality. Aristotle has a mathematical formula for reaching the right measure that constitutes justice, and therefore justice is very much about quantity and numbers. Justice implies also rectification of injustice done, or rectification of the wrong distribution of funds. He explains that a judge can restore equality and the right proportion and serve as an intermediary.

For Aquinas, justice indicates a certain kind of equality, and he holds the object of justice to be what is right and just. Justice implies doing good and avoiding evil. He too distinguishes between commutative justice, which concerns relations between individuals, and distributive justice, which concerns the political community.

Student: Is Aristotle building on previous views of justice?

Teacher: Aristotle mentions the Pythagoreans as defining justice as reciprocity with others. However, Aristotle states that reciprocity is not always the best solution to rectify an evil that has been perpetrated.

Student: His treatment of justice seems very different from that of Plato.

Teacher: Yes, and he gives many examples of justice, instead of searching for one definition, and he also thinks of different kinds of virtue, as we have seen.

Student: There appear to be many links between justice, on the one hand, and the law and politics on the other.

Teacher: Yes, because someone has to decide on the distribution of goods or the redress of some evil. Aristotle mentions currency as having the potentiality to equalize things, as a measure. Justice employs the law to redress evils, in cases where injustice is possible.

Student: How is justice a mean between extremes, according to Aristotle?

Teacher: The extremes would consist in possessing too much or too little, which respectively corresponds to doing injustice and suffering injustice. He also claims that justice is an intermediate condition, and injustice is in the extremes. The distribution of goods should take place between oneself and others, and between others. Justice and injustice imply a deliberate decision, and this is also the case when one gives oneself too many goods.

Student: Aristotle also mentions political justice.

Teacher: Yes, and political justice implies sharing a common life and being self-sufficient, free and having some kind of equality. The just political ruler does not award himself too many goods and works in the service of others and the community. That which is politically just must go hand in hand with the law.

Student: Is there justice in smaller communities?

Teacher: Aristotle mentions justice within the household. He also distinguishes between natural and legal justice. The former is the same everywhere and the latter is more particular, and it is something that people establish by convention.

Student: What are the similarities between natural and legal justice?

Teacher: They are both changeable, but that which is conventional is like an established measure, in the same way that the political systems can vary. At this point, Aristotle stresses the notion that an unjust act is done voluntarily, otherwise it is not unjust. It has to be up to the agent and done knowingly, more specifically knowing the object, the goal and the instrument. Unjust acts must be both voluntary and done knowingly, and if caused by the decision of the agent, he is unjust.

Like other virtues, justice requires effort and consequently it is not easy to become just. In addition, the just person knows how to be just and unjust, and the difference between them.

According to Aquinas, legal justice implies that the acts of all the virtues are directed to the common good.

He also states that one does not become unjust by executing only one unjust act.

Student: We have seen that virtue involves knowledge and decision, and so it makes sense to assume that the virtuous person must be able to distinguish between right and wrong with regard to each virtue.

Teacher: Precisely, all virtues involve knowledge, even the moral virtues.

Student: Does Aristotle discuss other moral virtues?

Teacher: Yes, he mentions decency, which is related to justice.

Student: Is it different from justice?

Teacher: Aristotle appears to consider it a superior form of justice, and it makes up for any shortcoming of the laws.

Student: Aristotle goes on to discuss the virtues of thought, correct?

Teacher: Yes, but first it would be good for us to analyze the moral virtues according to Aquinas.

Student: It seems that in Aristotle's works some virtues build on one another and they seem to be closely interrelated.

Teacher: Yes, magnificence is closely related to generosity, as we have seen, and for every virtue, being good towards others is a basic concept.

Student: Perhaps some of Aristotle's moral virtues are more important or fundamental than others?

Teacher: We can certainly think of some as more important than others, like justice in relation to wit, although Aristotle does not seem to propose a hierarchy of the moral virtues. Aquinas explains the order of treatment of the moral virtues in the *Nicomachean Ethics* in his commentary on this work. He states that first the virtues which concern internal passions are treated, such as courage and temperance, dealing with fear and desire. Subsequently, Aristotle examines virtues pertaining to secondary passions and external goods, such as generosity and magnanimity, going on to treat the virtues which concern external actions, such as justice.

In general, it is not clear that there is a limited number of virtues or that there should be a hierarchy. Aristotle bases his analysis on the character of a good man according to his principles.

Student: However, the cardinal virtues were considered by many philosophers to be central among the moral virtues?

Teacher: Yes, and we certainly should analyze what subsequent philosophers had to say about the cardinal virtues.

Student: Aquinas distinguishes the moral from the intellectual virtues.

Teacher: That is right, and it seems that he considers the moral virtues to be the virtues in the proper sense of the word. The speculative habits consider that which does not change and in that sense they do not change the appetitive part of the soul. They perfect the intellect, for instance in the contemplation of the truth, and they are virtues in that sense, but they do not immediately lead to the correct use of a habit. Aquinas states that if one makes correct use of what one knows, this is due to the will, which means that it is the moral virtues which permit the right use of knowledge.

Student: That is naturally very different from the position of Socrates or that of the Stoics?

Teacher: Yes, because for Socrates, knowledge should immediately translate into action, the only obstacle to virtue being ignorance. But Aquinas, and Aristotle before him, have a different position on virtue, and think of all kinds of inclinations, more or less rational, as interfering with the activity of the intellect. There is a certain degree of intellectualism in Aquinas, in the way that the will and the intellect work in tandem, and the will is defined as rational appetite. It represents a power and an act. However, the will clearly has a kind of autonomy which it does not seem to have for Socrates or Plato.

Student: I find it interesting that Aquinas considers the good work of the intellect or the good practical results of the intellect to be due to the moral virtues, which are in this way more complex and even more complete than the intellectual virtues. Could this be due to the Christian context in which he is writing?

Teacher: Yes, and obviously orthodox Christians do not believe that knowledge is the most important factor for being a good Christian and for salvation, a position that is very clear in the New Testament. However, Aristotle also explains that the virtues are divided according to the parts of the intellect, theoretical and practical. Within the intellect, the scientific and the calculating parts respectively consider the things that we cannot change and those that we can change. Aristotle mentions thought that is not concerned with action, and thought that is concerned with action and can lead to decision, through deliberative desire. He also states that moral virtue implies decision, as we have seen. However, there is a connection between knowledge and choice, for the right decision depends on true reason and deliberative desire, and desire follows upon the truth perceived. In that way, perception of the truth is not completely dissociated from action, although it does not directly lead to it. Decision relies on thought.

Student: And there is also thought about action, according to Aristotle.

Teacher: Exactly, and that kind of thought is the one leading to action.

Student: I understand how Aquinas was influenced by Aristotle on this issue, too.

Teacher: Absolutely, and Aquinas quotes all kinds of theological and philosophical sources, and accepts all kinds of influences, although the Christian matrix is very much the dominant influence.

Student: The relation between the intellect, the will and the passions could go some way towards explaining why some people who know the difference between right and wrong still do the wrong thing.

Teacher: Yes, this phenomenon has to be accounted for. Naturally, when it comes to action, there must be a connection between the intellect, theoretical and practical, and also the emotions and the appetitive part of the soul. The practical faculty concerns external work, rather than the speculative work of the intellect. For Aquinas, the sensitive appetite, which should follow reason, must be perfected by a habit making it agree with reason. Consequently, continence and perseverance, which allow one to withstand pleasures and pains, are not considered virtues in themselves, since the appetite should not incline one to illicit pleasures in the first place. The incontinent person is prone to certain passions which should not be there to start with.

Student: Are there reasons for knowing the right principle and not following it, according to Aquinas?

Teacher: One may and should know the universal principle of not doing evil. However, this knowledge can be impaired in particular cases by a passion.

Student: Is it possible that the universal principle is known, but somehow one thinks that the particular case does not fit the universal principle?

Teacher: That is also possible. Yet for Aquinas, moral virtue removes the obstacle of the illicit passions. Although the passions are involved in the practice of virtue, they are not virtues. They represent a movement of the sensitive appetite, but virtue is the principle of that movement, as a habit that is directed towards good. The passions are not good or evil, except in reference to reason. They should obey reason. They are also distinguished by Aquinas in the way that virtue begins in the reason and terminates in the appetite, and it is the other way around with the passions, which begin in the appetite.

Student: With regard to virtue, Aquinas accepts the principles laid out by Aristotle for virtuous action and character?

Teacher: Yes, and generally speaking, he states that a good life is based on good deeds. For him as for Aristotle, the way in which the action is done is important, and it must be based on right choice, following counsel, both of which, counsel and choice, are acts pertaining to reason, and directed to the end. We have seen that prudence considers the means to the end. Moral virtue consists in choosing the rational mean, and one's morals are defined by traits of character rather than one's intelligence.

Student: Aquinas makes distinctions between intellectual and moral virtues, but does he also find similarities?

Teacher: Yes. We will look into his conception of the intellectual virtues more closely later, but he thinks of a kind of correspondence in both cases. In the same way that the truth in the case of the speculative or theoretical intellect consists in the correspondence between the intellect and its object, the truth of the practical intellect consists in the correspondence between the practical intellect and right appetite.

Student: That would be an internal agreement, between the intellect and the will or the appetite generally speaking?

Teacher: Yes, and acts of reason are always involved when it comes to virtue, namely through counsel, which is a kind of inquiry, judgment, which is effected by the speculative intellect, and the command that issues from the practical intellect, and which is perfected by prudence.

Student: It is interesting to see how prudence, although it is associated with reason for Aquinas, also relies on other faculties of the soul.

Teacher: Yes, prudence relies on memory, understanding ('intelligentia') and foresight ('providentia'), for its activity.

Student: Is habit also an important element within the intellectual virtues, according to Aquinas?

Teacher: For both moral and intellectual virtues, habit is central. There is a habit of intellectual virtue in the same way as the habit of the moral virtues.

Student: It seems that the moral virtues play a central role for Aquinas, as we have seen. Do they require the intellectual virtues?

Teacher: Aquinas states that moral virtue requires understanding and prudence. Understanding includes the natural understanding of principles, for instance the universal principle of action to the effect that one should not do evil. Understanding means that we know the self-evident principles pertaining to speculative and practical matters. Prudence is also important given its essential link with the practical intellect and the fact that it is required for choosing the means towards the end of an action. However, Aquinas states that moral virtue does not necessarily require wisdom, science or art.

5.2. The Cardinal Virtues

Student: Aquinas thinks of the cardinal virtues as the main moral virtues, but these are not the only moral virtues, correct?

Teacher: That is right, he considered other virtues, even those that are not described by Aristotle.

Student: What are some of those virtues?

Teacher: He distinguishes moral virtues that are about operations and those that are about passions. Among the moral virtues that are about operations he includes religion and piety. He believes that justice is about operations and it is essentially about giving people their due, more specifically giving each person his or her due. And each moral virtue contains this aspect of justice, namely to give someone his or her due.

Student: Piety is the subject of Plato's *Euthyphro*.

Teacher: Yes, and it concerns our relationship with the divine. For Aquinas, these are special forms of justice. Religion means to pay one's debt to God, and piety consists in paying one's debt to one's parents. Gratitude means to pay our debt to our benefactors. Aquinas also distinguishes a general kind of justice which seeks the common good, and special justice which benefits an individual. In so far as the virtues seek the common good, they are associated with justice. Aquinas argues that prudence, as well as temperance and courage, can refer to the common good.

Student: Aquinas also includes several virtues under those that concern the passions, does he not?

Teacher: That is correct, and we have already seen that courage or fortitude concern the irascible faculty and temperance regulates the concupiscible faculty. Aquinas includes magnanimity among these kinds of passions and considers it to be about hope and despair. Equally, reason and the sensitive appetite have their roles to play, but the perfection of virtue comes from reason, while the perfection of the passions depends on the appetite. For Aquinas, the moral virtues listed by Aristotle in the *Nicomachean Ethics* are all about the passions, except for justice. Different passions concern different virtues, since the passions bear different relations to reason. However, different objects of the same kind of operation have the same relation to reason.

Student: Does he mention how the virtues are differentiated?

Teacher: Aquinas states that they are differentiated according to the different goods that are pursued and obtainable, for instance, pertaining to the body or the soul, or to one's relation to other people. For instance, temperance concerns a good that is discerned by the sense of touch, which according to Aquinas is particularly intense, including eating and drinking. It concerns the goods of the body, which should be enjoyed in moderation. For Aquinas as for Aristotle, virtue is about difficult things.

Student: It is interesting to see how virtue, for Aristotelian philosophers, is based on nature but it is also something difficult to obtain.

Teacher: Virtue is something that is within us to achieve, and in that sense it is something natural. However, it is something that is potentially in us and that has to be practiced and developed with the aid of reason, and in conformity with reason.

Aquinas adds that what is natural can refer to the individual nature or the specific nature, that of the species, and virtue is natural in both senses. According to him, the human will has a natural inclination or appetite for the good, in accordance with reason. Individually, some individuals may be more inclined to particular virtues, intellectual or moral. We do not have perfect virtue to start with, but we can achieve it through habit and practice.

Student: And virtue is also something that we can perfect and that perfects us?

Teacher: Yes, we can become more virtuous through practice and subsequently virtue makes us better.

Like Aristotle, Aquinas thinks of virtue as a mean, or the agreement with a certain measure or rule. Moral virtue should follow the rule of reason. Keeping to the mean indicates such conformity and equality.

Student: Is observing the mean also true for the intellectual virtues? It would seem that the more we know, the better.

Teacher: Aquinas states that knowledge consists in the conformity of the intellect with its object, and the object is the rule and the mean, resulting in truth, or true knowledge. In that sense, the rule of the mean is observed in relation to the intellectual virtues, as well as the moral virtues. The mean of moral virtue is rectitude of reason. This indicates that in the case of the intellectual virtues it is not a question of more or less, excess or deficiency, but hitting the target precisely.

Student: Is the mean also observed in the theological virtues?

Teacher: No. In this case, a maximum of charity, for instance, is to be sought, and the mean is not observed. Perhaps because these virtues are not specifically Aristotelian, Aquinas feels free to deviate from the rule of the mean with respect to these virtues. Accordingly, there is no excess in these virtues. We can always love God more, and have greater faith and hope in Him. We can think of the intellectual virtues as a mean or midpoint in the sense of understanding the truth exactly, as he states in the *Disputed Questions on Virtue*.

Student: Does Aquinas also believe in the unity of the virtues?

Teacher: He holds that imperfect moral virtue consists in an inclination to do a good deed, but perfect moral virtue implies the connection between the virtues. Perfect virtue implies the presence of the virtues together. In addition, prudence and the moral virtues imply each other. In the same way, certain virtues have certain properties. Prudence includes discretion, justice includes rectitude, temperance includes moderation and courage includes strength of mind. True prudence also involves the other cardinal virtues, and these in turn require prudence. Because prudence concerns the choice of the means, it must be present in the practice of the other cardinal virtues. Aquinas also states in the *Summa Theologiae* that the rule of prudence covers the entire matter of the moral virtues. For one to be virtuous, one has to exercise oneself in the matters of all moral virtues.

Student: Is this also true for the intellectual virtues?

Teacher: Aquinas believes that the objects of the intellectual virtues may not necessarily be connected, and therefore the link between the intellectual virtues is not as close as that which can be found within the moral virtues and the cardinal virtues. However, all the intellectual virtues rely on the understanding of universal principles. Equally, these principles do not depend on the conclusions. With regard to the moral virtues, reason moves the appetite and the appetite moves reason, and therefore the connection between these virtues is much tighter.

Student: And Aquinas believes that the moral virtues are the typical human virtues?

Teacher: That is true, since perfect virtue implies rectitude of the appetite and confers the ability to do well and produces good work. He adds that there is imperfect virtue which does not cause good work or the good deed done. However, the principal virtues are the cardinal virtues. Among the cardinal virtues, Aquinas considers prudence, as an act of reason, to be an intellectual virtue, but with a close affinity to the moral virtues. He describes as justice the use of reason in relation to something else. Temperance ensures control of the passions which incline to something against reason, and the passions which induce us not to follow reason because of fear are controlled by courage. Because only prudence resides in the intellect as an intellectual virtue, the other virtues are rational by participation. The subject of justice is the will, as rational appetite, while temperance is in the concupiscible faculty and courage or fortitude is in the irascible faculty, as we have seen. The temperate person is not just self-controlled but rather does not have disordered sensual desires.

Student: Does Aquinas explain why these virtues are called 'cardinal', as being the fundamental ones?

Teacher: Aquinas states that they are more general than the other virtues. Prudence concerns general good rational judgment in acting, or producing the good as a result of rational consideration. Justice produces the good in operations concerning the good or what is right and due. Temperance in general curbs the passions, and courage strengthens the mind against passions. These virtues are also called cardinal because of the importance of their matter. Prudence, generally speaking, commands, while justice concerns the right actions between equals. Temperance controls desires related to the sense of touch, and fortitude strengthens us against the fear of death, and strengthens the mind against the passions. He considers all these aspects central for moral life.

Student: Are the cardinal virtues essentially about human matters?

Teacher: Aquinas states that the cardinal virtues can also serve to direct us to God. Prudence can include the contemplation of God and things divine, and the other cardinal virtues may also have divine things as their final goal, instead of earthly concerns.

Student: And for Aquinas, the end of virtue is also happiness, is it not?

Teacher: Yes, but he distinguishes happiness that can be obtained by us, and a kind of happiness which surpasses human nature, and which requires the theological virtues. We have seen that these virtues are infused by God and their object is God, and they are made known to us by revelation. He considers the infused virtues to be the perfect ones because their goal is the ultimate end. In the *Disputed Questions on Virtue*, he also distinguishes between the happiness of contemplation as a virtuous activity, and the happiness of action which relies on the activity of practical reason.

Student: Does Aquinas define perfect virtue?

Teacher: He states that it consists in doing well what is good, thus producing the good in the right way. He states that, strictly speaking, virtue is a perfection, but it can be understood more broadly as consisting in what is good in human acts and passions.

Student: We have seen that some philosophers value some virtues over others. Does Aquinas have a hierarchy of virtues?

Teacher: Among the cardinal virtues, prudence surpasses the other moral virtues because it perfects reason, which is the cause of our good as human beings. Then comes justice, which resides in the will, as rational appetite. Justice is superior to the other moral virtues because it essentially benefits other persons. Courage participates more in reason than does temperance and therefore it surpasses temperance. For him virtue can amount to more or less in different people, at different times, and it may include a greater natural disposition or habituation.

Student: According to Aquinas, is it possible to possess perfect virtue?

Teacher: With regard to virtue in general, he says that for the Stoics virtue consists in a maximum, but Aquinas himself does not think that one has to have perfect virtue in order to be virtuous; it is sufficient to approach the mean of right reason. Perhaps in a more Platonic sense, he holds that the subject can participate more or less in virtue. In this way we can compare the virtues among themselves or compare the degree of virtue in each of us. In terms of the object, Aquinas advances the view that given the closer connection of the intellectual virtues with reason, they can be said to be superior to the moral virtues, which perfect the appetite, rather than reason. In terms of action, the moral virtues are naturally superior, because virtue consists in being a principle of action. The superiority of certain virtues over others depends on one's point of view.

Student: Aristotle appears to prefer justice as the main moral virtue.

Teacher: Yes, and for Aquinas justice is also the main moral virtue, followed by courage and temperance. Prudence is superior to the moral virtues, as an intellectual virtue. Prudence goes along with the practical intellect, while the other moral virtues perfect the passions.

Student: Is prudence the most important intellectual virtue?

Teacher: Aquinas holds wisdom to be the most important intellectual virtue, above prudence and the other intellectual virtues, because it contemplates the supreme cause, namely, God. The object of a virtue determines its greatness. This object is also more certain than any other object, and Aquinas follows Aristotle in saying that it is better to know a little about greater things than to know much about inferior things.

Student: I understand that Aquinas has a comprehensive view of the virtues, in trying to unite all the traditions that come before him, such as the Platonic, the Aristotelian and the Stoic traditions, while taking into account Augustine's views. With regard to the virtues he closely follows Aristotle's position, but he accepts Augustine's definition of virtue, and he develops the theory of the theological virtues. All virtues are closely connected. Moreover, he develops the theory of the infused moral virtues, in addition to the theological virtues, which can only be infused by God and cannot be naturally acquired.

I wonder if the moral virtues and the intellectual virtues will remain in the afterlife?

Teacher: The moral virtues will be present in a perfect way, in accordance with reason. There will be no occasions for the virtues to fail, such as fear of death, and one's appetite will be perfectly in conformity with reason. The intellectual virtues will also remain in the afterlife. Aquinas states, based on the story of Lazarus as recounted in the New Testament, that we will have knowledge of particular events in the next life. Universal knowledge is more stable and we will therefore also possess that knowledge in the next life.

Student: We have looked into the question of the moral virtues as they are conceived by Aristotle and Aquinas. If we think of the exemplars who practice these virtues, we can perhaps find some differences.

It seems to me that some of the virtues described by Aristotle might be specific to the ancient Greek society in which Aristotle lived.

Teacher: Yes, several scholars have noted that virtues like magnificence and magnanimity befit a certain kind of person. Not everyone has the kind of wealth to exercise these virtues. Perhaps because Aristotle thinks of a free adult male as the possible culmination of human nature, certain virtues are reserved for that kind of person.

Student: Plato and the Stoics have a more universal conception of the virtues.

Teacher: Yes, and we must note the similarities between the Stoics and Plato, or at least between Socrates as he explains the virtues in the Platonic dialogues and the Stoics. We also find that the Christian model of virtue is quite different from that of Aristotle.

Student: We have seen that the theological virtues are specific to Christian writers.

Teacher: That is correct, and in the Middle Ages we find an emphasis on voluntary poverty which is significant and would have no parallel in Aristotle, who emphasizes that wealth can provide the opportunity to exercise a virtue that less well-off people are unable to practice, since external means are required.

Student: The medieval Christian model of the virtuous person is quite different, then?

Teacher: Absolutely. We have seen that there are many similarities between Aristotle and Aquinas when it comes to broad features of virtue. Both think of virtue as a mean between two extremes, as the result of habituation and as leading to happiness. It is also clear that Aquinas provides a definition of virtue and of the various virtues by using Aristotelian vocabulary, in particular the categories. Aquinas also includes the understanding of virtue according to the Christian tradition, and does not stop at the Aristotelian virtues; neither is he encumbered by the historical context in which Aristotle writes. He thinks of humility as indirectly supporting all the virtues, and humility does not seem to feature in some of the virtues described by Aristotle, although it is implied, for instance, in truthfulness.

Student: The medieval Christian virtuous person would likely be a saint?

Teacher: Yes, and she or he would have the theological virtues, which are absent from Aristotle.

Student: You have also mentioned the significance of poverty.

Teacher: The virtues of the medieval man or woman also have to be understood in their historical context. We find the rise of religious orders in Europe, and the question of poverty becomes particularly prominent with the birth of the mendicant orders in Europe in the early 13th century, including the Dominican order, to which Aquinas belonged. This new kind of religious order stirred a controversy, although these orders were ultimately accepted by the central powers of the Church, more specifically, the Pope.

Student: And the model of the virtuous person was the saint, who tended to be a religious person, belonging to a religious order?

Teacher: Exactly, and people belonging to religious orders were expected to obey the three vows of poverty, chastity and obedience. Poverty was certainly considered a virtue. Chastity implied the abstinence from certain kinds of pleasures, and obedience implied giving up one's personal will.

Student: That would not mean obeying bad orders?

Teacher: No, obviously not, one's sense of right and wrong should remain intact. However, with regard to the variations in the conception of virtue, it is important to take the context into account. Certain features of virtue are universal among our philosophers, but one certainly finds important adaptations according to the historical as well as the political and the religious context.

In the *Summa Theologica*, Aquinas discusses religious and secular aspects of the virtues alternately, and he does not make a stark distinction between a religious or a secular approach to virtue. These two aspects are not separable, in his view. The same kind of virtue can be developed by us or given to us by God, such as moral justice and infused justice, as we have seen. In addition, he considers different virtues as associated with justice, for instance religion and piety, but also gratitude and truthfulness, as an example of his merging of religious and secular virtues. For him, religion is a special virtue in itself, and it directs us to God.

Student: I understand that for Aquinas the secular and the religious or theological aspects of the virtues are intertwined.

We have mentioned the links between ethics and politics, and the way in which Aristotle does not think of them separately, but views ethics and the way we deal with each other as belonging also, as a stepping stone, to the discussion of politics.

Teacher: Yes, but as we have seen the question of politics is much more structural, involving the way human society is organized and managed. In that sense, it is more complex than ethics, whose end concerns individual human behavior. Ethics, in particular that which is called normative ethics, seeks general rules that all individuals can follow, even if one could contemplate societal or structural virtues.

Student: Perhaps ethics and political theory imply one another?

Teacher: Yes, politics certainly requires ethics, since it rests on the assumption that individuals will act in the right way and according to right reason. That kind of behavior is necessary in order to contribute to the common good. In the same way, it is difficult to think of ethics as completely separate from politics, since, as Aristotle says, human beings are political animals. There is also a close connection between ethics and virtue in Plato, particularly in the *Republic*, in the sense that the virtues of the different classes are also present in different parts of the soul. Human society reflects the different parts of the soul, and the virtues of the different parts of the soul are also present in the different parts of society, more specifically, in the different classes of people.

Student: Yes, and as we have seen, Shaftesbury also holds that social activities are the most natural and appropriate for human beings, the most virtuous and the ones that will make us happier.

Teacher: Certainly, it is difficult to separate in principle ethics and politics although each of them is a very broad field, and therefore we will have to focus on ethics, and particularly on virtue ethics.

Student: However, perhaps we could examine some political implications of virtue? Should virtue be imposed by society or the laws? Should there be a political system which actively encourages virtuous behavior?

Teacher: That is a very interesting question, and one that comes up already in the writings of Plato. Naturally, that question cannot be dissociated from the issue of education. In the Middle Ages, there are commentaries on Plato's *Republic*, for instance, by medieval or classical Islamic philosophers, who expand on the link between virtue, education and politics, naturally within an Islamic context.

Student: And obviously for these philosophers it is important for the state to prescribe the kind of education which will foster virtuous behavior?

Teacher: Yes, and especially among the young. This principle is also present in Aristotle.

Student: Perhaps there can be an approach to education towards virtue which does not impose from above, but promotes the individual quest for virtuous behavior based on free choice, and free will in general.

Teacher: That is possible, although several authors who followed Plato on the question of education for virtuous behavior were not in favor of democracy, which they viewed as an individualistic and chaotic political system. For instance, Alfarabi, in his major work, *The Principles of the Opinions of the Virtuous City*, clearly favors a kind of political system which is led, as in Plato, by a philosopher who, for Alfarabi, is also a religious leader. It is clear that education is controlled by the state, which oversees the quest for the common good in the virtuous city. The main values are spiritual rather than material. In his commentary on Plato's *Republic*, Averroes, following Plato's ideas, is quite explicit on the education of the youth in virtuous behavior.

Student: If those plans were to be strictly followed, the result would in principle be very positive, that is to say, if everyone were to work towards the common good.

Teacher: Yes, if both rulers and the majority of people have the common good in mind, in their intentions and actions, the outcome ought to be positive.

Student: The idea of virtue can certainly be abused for political motives at certain moments in time. During the

French Revolution, Robespierre's motto 'virtue or terror' certainly seems like an imposition and an abuse of power. Perhaps an encouragement through the laws and the example of political leaders rather than the imposition of virtuous practices is to be favored from a political point of view.

Teacher: I agree, although in Plato's, and also in Alfarabi's and Averroes' works, the notion of a utopia is very much present. They are clearly not describing a state that actually existed in their lifetimes or before. Naturally the role of virtue within the political state is very broad and would require a detailed discussion.

Student: We have also mentioned a possible connection between the laws and virtue.

Teacher: Yes, and in the *Nicomachean Ethics*, Aristotle states that the law can command one to be virtuous, for instance, to be courageous (not to abandon a battle) or to be temperate (not to commit adultery).

5.3. Friendship

Student: On the question of virtue and personal relationships, Aristotle devotes two books of the *Nicomachean Ethics* to friendship, more than to any single virtue, moral or intellectual.

Teacher: Friendship is a very important topic. Friendship is a virtue or accompanies virtue; it seems to be a coronation of the virtues. For Aquinas, it is the result of virtue, and for him, charity is a kind of friendship with God.

Student: How significant is friendship within ethical theory?

Teacher: Friendship is very important in general and an unavoidable topic within ethics because it concerns our relationship with others in a way that can be characterized as morally correct or incorrect treatment. It is a debate that belongs definitely within the discussion of ethics, and also virtue.

Student: Could it simply be a part of ethics and not related to virtue?

Teacher: Friendship is not a moral duty, and the highest form of friendship is not for pleasure or utility but a way of exercising the virtues, and in that sense, friendship is definitely part of the discussion of virtue ethics.

Student: What does it mean to say that friendship is not a moral duty?

Teacher: Friendship can be studied from different perspectives, as we shall see, but some philosophers do not think it is something necessary. We can live with others and help one another without necessarily being friends with them. Friendship requires a certain kind of familiarity, and companionship that is not enjoined upon us, but seems to indicate something over and above the virtue of benevolence. In fact, friendship appears to accompany many virtues.

Student: In some of his works, Rousseau does not seem to think of friendship as something necessary.

Teacher: That is correct. In the *Discourse on the Origin of Inequality*, he thinks that human beings are happiest and more virtuous when they are by themselves. They only get together to form families and communities in other to obtain safety and security.

Student: Is this a prevalent opinion in Rousseau?

Teacher: When we read other works, including the *Confessions*, we see that he personally values friendship, even if this is not always apparent in some of his works.

Student: Aristotle has a detailed treatment of friendship in the *Nicomachean Ethics*.

Teacher: Exactly, he devotes great attention to this topic. Friendship had already been discussed by Plato in his dialogues, including *Lysis* and the *Symposium*, but Aristotle is more systematic. Later, there are other works devoted to this topic, for instance, by Cicero. Aristotle states that friendship is necessary for life, since no one would like to be without friends. For one thing, it is an occasion to practice virtue in works of beneficence.

Student: When Aristotle says that it is necessary, it does not mean that it is based on utility, is that correct?

Teacher: That is right, although that is one kind of friendship which is also important. The highest kind of friendship is the one based on virtue. He thinks of friendship not only as something useful but also good in itself.

Student: Aristotle has a broad conception of friendship, does he not?

Teacher: He does, and he thinks of friendship in ways that are not immediately obvious to us; for instance, he mentions a natural friendship between parents and their children. This is also possible among us, but it is something that is possibly different from the natural bond between parent and child as we conceive it. And in Aristotle's time, children were considered to be the property of the parents, and therefore the relationship between parents and children would have been more formal than the current one, when children tend to have more rights.

Student: Aristotle assumes that friendship is something natural?

Teacher: Yes, he thinks that friendship derives or is related to a certain affinity among species. He finds this affinity to exist within a species, and in particular, human beings.

Student: In that case, he also assumes that human beings are naturally good to one another?

Teacher: Yes, there is that kind of affinity binding a species, and he finds that this is especially the case among human beings.

Student: Perhaps that is due to the fact that we have more complex organized societies than other animals, and opportunities for showing that affinity or friendship are more common.

Teacher: That sounds plausible. Friendship comes from this natural affinity with beings who are similar to us, and it is a feeling that binds together members of the same species. For Aristotle, in so far as it consists in a kind of harmony and concord, friendship can be considered even more important than justice, in the eyes of legislators. Justice in this sense serves to correct an evil, and friendship would preempt that kind of need. Friends would naturally avoid injustice.

Student: Aristotle also studies which kind of people are friends, does he not?

Teacher: He does, and part of the inquiry is about whether people who are not virtuous can truly be friends, and how many kinds of friendship there are.

Student: He thinks of affinity as closely related to friendship and a strong component of friendship. Does he also mention the object of friendship?

Teacher: As we have seen, friendship is a virtue or associated with virtue. It also bears many similarities with other ethical issues. In friendship, we seek that which is good. We love that which is worthy of love, or lovable, and Aristotle thinks that what is sought in a friendship falls into three categories, the useful, the pleasant, and the good. The useful is a means to an end, but the pleasant and the good are ends in themselves. He also asks the question whether people love the good in itself or what is good for them, and remarks that these two kinds of good do not always coincide. One is naturally attracted to what is good for oneself.

Student: He also mentions the difference between the good and that which appears to be good.

Teacher: That is right, and we always seek that which seems good to us.

Student: He then mentions the good, the pleasant and the useful as causes of love?

Teacher: That is correct, and these also constitute three kinds of friendship. Another important component of friendship is benevolence. We wish our friends well, and this does not include inanimate beings.

Student: That makes sense, since friendship is based on affinity, and inanimate beings do not perceive, in general, or reciprocate our friendship.

Teacher: Precisely, and Aristotle also states that friendship is based on mutual goodwill, otherwise it is merely goodwill.

Student: However, we often have goodwill towards people we do not know, such as, for instance, certain public figures.

Teacher: That is correct, and that is why Aristotle states that friendship must include the awareness of this mutual goodwill.

Student: And for that to happen, surely, friends must be in frequent contact?

Teacher: That is definitely the case. Many philosophers mention regular acquaintance as a condition of friendship, and so does Aristotle, especially in the case of true friendship, the one based on virtue. Spending time with friends is an essential aspect of friendship.

Student: What is the difference between the three kinds of friendship mentioned by Aristotle?

Teacher: Only in friendship based on virtue do we value the friends for their own sake and truly wish them well. In the case of friendship for utility, the friend is rather a means to an end, and in the case of friendship for pleasure we love those friends for the pleasure of their company, rather than their character as a whole. For Aristotle, these are accidents, because we love these friends not in their entirety but for some particular characteristic. As a result, these kinds of friendship are not as stable as friendship based on virtue. He tends to associate friendship based on pleasure with younger people, and friendship based on utility as a characteristic of older people. Younger people appear to be more readily guided by feelings. Because of this Aristotle thinks it is easier to make friends among younger people.

Student: That still seems to be the case today. Perhaps this is because younger people are less choosy and more flexible and adaptable, and their personalities are still evolving.

Teacher: According to Aristotle, friendship at a young age is quicker to form and to dissolve.

Student: How does Aristotle describe the perfect kind of friendship?

Teacher: This kind of friendship is based on people's goodness and virtue, and in this kind of friendship one wishes one's friend good for him- or herself. Consequently, this kind of friendship is more stable. Interestingly, it also includes utility and pleasure, and therefore this is a complete kind of friendship. However, this kind of friendship is not as frequent as the other kinds, since it is difficult to find people who meet the criteria for being friends based on virtue.

Student: And one has to be thoroughly good in order to develop this complete kind of friendship?

Teacher: That is right. However, for the other two kinds of friendship, this perfect goodness is not required, and Aristotle accepts that bad people can develop friendships for pleasure and utility. However, in friendship based on virtue friends trust each other more and slander is less likely.

Student: Is friendship just between two people, or more?

Teacher: Aristotle also mentions friendship between cities, as a kind of friendship for utility, but friendship tends to develop typically between individuals for Aristotle. Obviously, today we think of friendship primarily as something that develops between two people. True friendship is the one based on virtue and goodness. It also requires regular common activities, as we have seen, and Aristotle emphasizes this aspect to the point of saying that friends should live together.

Student: Why does Aristotle say that only friendship based on virtue is true?

Teacher: Basically, because in true friendship we love our friends for what they are, but in the other kinds of friendship we seek them because of something they can provide, such as something pleasant or useful. This distinction is in line with Aristotle's differentiation between substance and accidents. Friendship should be based on someone's character, not something accidental to the friend, as is the case with friendship for pleasure or utility.

Student: Aristotle states that friendship is a state rather than a feeling, such as loving.

Teacher: That is correct, he thinks of friendship as something more stable than a feeling, and as something that requires decision, which issues from a state. In the perfect kind of friendship, we wish friends well, more than in the imperfect kinds of friendship, even if Aristotle thinks that we first wish goods to ourselves. Friendship also requires us to know our friends well, which means spending time with them. The more perfect the friendship, the more difficult it is to have it with many people.

Student: Is there a difference of rank between the imperfect kinds of friendship?

Teacher: Aristotle views friendship for pleasure as more genuine than friendship for utility, because it shows a greater kind of equality, and equality is also a hallmark of true friendship. Friends for utility do not necessarily spend time together either. In addition, friendship based on virtue also tends to include the pleasant.

Student: Does friendship always imply equality?

Teacher: One also finds friendship between unequal people, such as the friendship between father and son, and Aristotle also mentions friendships with someone superior in power, and between older and younger people, or men and women, whom he does not consider to be equal. All these constitute different kinds of friendship. The superior partner should be more loved, and this would restore some equality to the friendship.

Student: Are there other types of inequality?

Teacher: Yes, for instance inequality in virtue or wealth, and also in power. This raises an interesting question, which is whether we wish friends the kind of good that will change their nature and position, for instance, wishing that friends become gods, which would be tantamount to desiring the greatest good for them. Gods, however, do not need friends, and therefore the friendship would be lost, according to Aristotle.

Student: How does he solve that problem?

Teacher: He states that we love friends for what they are, not for what they can become. In addition, such radical change would put an end to the friendship and therefore it is not desirable, for a good would be lost.

Aristotle also states that friendship is about giving and receiving. He remarks that because many people love honor, they prefer to be loved than to love.

Student: However, Aristotle states that loving is better than to love.

Teacher: Naturally, since being active is better than passivity. These are people who love honor, and also love flatterers, someone who pretends to be a friend but is not.

Student: Are these not different kinds of honor?

Teacher: Yes, and other philosophers later mention this, too. Some like to be honored because they hope to get something from those who honor them, especially if the latter are more powerful. If one is honored for one's goodness, then it comes as confirmation of one's good character, which is a good thing. For Aristotle, friendship is more about loving than being loved, and he gives the example of mothers, who are happy just to love and to see to the welfare of their children.

Student: He states that loving is the virtue of friends.

Teacher: Loving is the activity of friends, and it can smooth over any inequality. Affinity and similarities are very important in forming and maintaining friendships. Friends can be equal in virtue, even if they are not equal in other respects. As result, in this kind of friendship, the friends do not wrong each other and they do not ask their friends to do something that is wrong.

Student: What other types of inequality are possible among friends?

Teacher: According to Aristotle, friendship for utility is the one where inequality is mostly found, and it allows for friendship between those who are poor and those who are rich, or those who are knowledgeable and those who are not.

Student: Would not virtue restore equality even in these cases?

Teacher: Perhaps this is not possible, according to Aristotle, since he thinks that only wealthy people can possess certain virtues, such as magnificence. This is part of his understanding of the part external goods play in the practice of virtue.

Student: Aristotle also compares friendship and justice.

Teacher: That is correct, although he says, when he begins to discuss friendship in the *Nicomachean Ethics*, that friendship dispenses with justice, given that, in principle, no wrongdoing is done among friends. At any rate, there is a close affinity between friendship and justice. He adds that communities involve justice and friendship, and friendship implies some kind of community.

Student: Is there a particular kind of community for the flourishing of friendship?

Teacher: Aristotle states that the community between brothers and companions is the closest one. The political kind of community aims at advantage and utility. He also mentions temporary types of communities, such as those among travelers, but these can be subsumed under the political community. In addition, he describes how friendship is present in the different kinds of political system, such as aristocracy, monarchy and democracy, as well as in families. However, in these cases, friendship and justice are closely connected and it is not as clear in which way friendship differs from justice.

With regard to justice, it may differ between parents and children, or among brothers. At the same time, the requirement of justice increases as the friendship is closer. For instance, Aristotle states that it is worse to rob a friend than to rob a stranger.

Student: I understand that friendship cannot include everyone, and that the number of friends that we can have should be limited. However, justice should be the same with regard to everyone. In that sense, justice would have a broader scope than friendship.

Teacher: That was perhaps not as obvious for Aristotle, in whose time children and women had fewer rights than adult males. In that sense friendship and justice were more closely related for him than is the case for us today. However, even today there can be an obligation of assistance, in particular towards relatives, since we are closer to them and have the ability to help them.

Student: Does Aristotle recognize friendship or justice in any kind of political community?

Teacher: There is only friendship or justice if there is a similarity between ruler and ruled. He does not acknowledge that similarity between master and slave, except in so far as the slave is a human being.

Student: This description of friendship in political communities says a lot about society and political rights in Aristotle's time, but perhaps less about friendship in general and how it develops today.

Teacher: That is right, since political rights have been extended, and slavery has been legally abolished. The notion of equality is stressed by Rousseau, but it was not always present before, as we know. A new radical notion of equality developed in the modern period.

Student: Aristotle also analyzes friendship within the family.

Teacher: He does, although in this case friendship seems to bear the general meaning of love, such as the love that binds parents and their children. This kind of love is based on affinity and proximity, and the way in which they are perceived. Because the mother is consciously aware of her children as her product, she loves them before they love her, and equally, she loves them more than does the father.

Student: However, the parents love their children owing to the affinities between them, do they not?

Teacher: Yes, the father sees his child as another self, whereas children love their parents as having come from them, and the common parentage unites the brothers.

Student: Are there other uniting factors?

Teacher: Being brought up together also unites siblings, as well as proximity in age and the similarity between them.

Student: Would this be a friendship based on virtue?

Teacher: Yes, and certainly Terence Irwin in his comments, as part of his English translation of the *Nicomachean Ethics*, holds that friendship within the family is based on virtue, since family members are loved for themselves rather than simply for utility or pleasure, although these elements are included. In addition, children love their parents in so far as these are superior to them, and the friendship between siblings is like that between companions.

Student: And this kind of friendship is natural?

Teacher: It is natural, including the friendship between husband and wife, which also includes utility and pleasure, as they divide their functions in working towards the common good. We must bear in mind that Aristotle's term for friendship, 'philia', has a broader meaning that our term 'friendship'.

Aristotle holds that the family is a more natural kind of community than the political community.

He praises in particular the friendship among good people, and states that friendship is a kind of equality, as we have seen. Complete friendship cannot be had with many people, and one should get to know one's friend well. It is possible to have more friends in the kind of friendship for utility or pleasure than within virtuous friendship.

Student: He also makes distinctions based on age.

Teacher: Yes, and that appears to imply that one's character and personality are also important. Friendship based on virtue is more harmonious and involves fewer frictions, unlike the friendship for utility. Aristotle says that one always requires more from one's friend.

Student: Friendship seems to have its own rules, does it not?

Teacher: Yes, and especially friendship for utility, which is based on the goods that are exchanged.

Student: Naturally, Aristotle privileges what is good over that which is useful?

Teacher: That is correct, and he even states that people aim at the good and fine, but then tend to incline to the beneficial. Friendship for utility includes rules for what one gives and receives, and it is more complex in that way. If there is a friendship between unequal friends, there is a dispute as to who should receive more, whether the superior party, because of his or her superiority, or the inferior party, because he or she has greater needs. Aristotle states that one is justified to assume that the superior person should receive more honor, and the other person should receive more profit, in order that each receives what befits them. This kind of arrangement would also apply within the political community. He seems to accept that one should receive honor or money, but not both.

Student: He also seems to assume that sometimes it is not possible to give our friends their due.

Teacher: That is correct, for instance in the case of one's relationship with one's parents and the gods. It is difficult to honor them as they deserve, or according to their worth. Aristotle also views exchange of goods, including pleasure, as part of friendship. A set of calculations is involved, although this is less likely in the friendship for virtue. He mentions the Sophists in this context, and seems to contemplate a kind of friendship between teachers and pupils.

Student: Aristotle does have a broad conception of friendship.

Teacher: That is right, and it includes romantic love. We have seen that before the books on friendship, within the *Nicomachean Ethics*, he discusses the virtue of friendliness, and friendship certainly is a stronger kind of attachment, but it can still be quite broadly understood. As a general rule, within a friendship we should do the favors that accord with the recipient of those favors, and according to the worth of our friends, their needs, and based on how close we are to them, while taking account of their age and rank.

Student: That seems to constitute another similarity between friendship and justice, and virtue more generally.

Teacher: Precisely, in the sense that one gives each person what they deserve or their due. And this includes respect for one's position and age.

Student: Does Aristotle also establish rules for dissolving friendships?

Teacher: He does, and he thinks that in the case of friendships for pleasure or utility it is acceptable to dissolve the friendship when pleasure or utility are no longer to be obtained. Interestingly, honesty is also important in friendships, in the sense that it should be clear to our friends on what grounds the friendship is based, and whether we love them for pleasure, utility or their character.

Student: It is also possible to dissolve a friendship based on virtue, is it not?

Teacher: Yes, Aristotle states that this is possible if our friends become vicious instead of being virtuous. In such a case, we should try to restore their character. However, if a friend clearly becomes more virtuous than he or she was before, that is not a reason for dissolving the friendship.

Student: The question of change must be taken into account in friendship, then?

Teacher: That is correct, because in friendships that begin in childhood, for instance, the changes are likely to be greater, as one's personality is being formed.

Another feature of true friendship is to wish the friends good for their own sake. Spending time with one's friends, and sharing their joys and sorrows, is very important. In other words, a friend wishes for her friend what she wishes for herself, and the friend is another self in the case of virtuous friends. Naturally, this kind of friendship is not for the majority of people, according to Aristotle. The good person enjoys his friend, and is at peace with him in the same way that he is at peace and in harmony with himself.

Student: This conception of friendship seems to resemble Plato's notion of virtue as a harmony within the soul.

Teacher: Precisely. The vicious person has a conflicted soul, and therefore that person does not wish to spend time with himself. The virtuous person has a soul that is in harmony with itself and values particularly the rational part of his soul. This person does not truly regret what he or she has done.

Student: It seems difficult to attain that kind of ideal.

Teacher: In principle, this state of mind is possible to achieve, but Aristotle does not think that it is possible for most people.

Student: That is understandable. The good is that which is loved, and the will tends to seek the good. People who are not good will not love themselves, because the object of the will in this case is not good. Aristotle also seems to think that we have to be good and pleasant in ourselves and to ourselves before we can be good to our friends.

Teacher: Those elements certainly go together.

Student: Aristotle thinks of friendship as a broad category since we can be friends with our parents, brothers, teachers, and perhaps even the gods. Does he also understand friendship in a more specific way?

Teacher: Absolutely. He does not believe that friendship is only about good will, since we can wish strangers well. Moreover, goodwill does not necessarily lead to action in favor of another. However, Aristotle states that goodwill can be the beginning of friendship, particularly in friendship based on virtue. Concord or unanimity, and agreement on a particular course of action, are also part of friendship, particularly political friendship.

Aristotle also mentions benefactors as important elements in friendship, and the importance of giving over receiving, since it is something active and fine. In the same way that he stresses the fact that doing others a good turn is important, he also mentions the issue of self-love.

Student: It would appear, in principle, that friendship is about helping others and that thinking about ourselves is something selfish, which should have no part in a friendship.

Teacher: Self-love is bad, according to Aristotle, when we wish to have external goods mainly for ourselves, like wealth and honor. These goods please primarily the nonrational part of the soul and are therefore relativized by Aristotle as being accessory rather than essential. If someone seeks what is fine and is temperate, he or she is not berated for self-love. However, Aristotle believes that this is what truly pertains to self-love, because, as is implied, one loves one's superior part, namely reason, which in this way controls the other parts of the soul. This kind of self-love, which is self-love properly speaking, is not objectionable.

Student: It is interesting to see how Aristotle always places the focus on reason and on being active, as truly essential human and good characteristics.

Teacher: That is apparent in many aspects of his philosophy, such as his metaphysics and physics, and then also in his ethics. He argues that voluntary actions are those involving reason. It is not surprising that he defines the human being as a rational animal, with an emphasis on the rational part, as what is distinctive of the human species.

Student: Is there a clear distinction between the two kinds of self-love, the good one and the objectionable one?

Teacher: The self-love is good when one is guided by reason, and the bad kind is when one is guided by feelings. According to Aristotle, there is no conflict between true self-love and virtue, since the person who strives for what is good and fine will necessarily work towards the common good. Equally, the virtuous person helps others while being good to him- or herself, since virtue brings benefit to the good person and to those around her. He had already said that the vicious person was conflicted and therefore not at ease with him- or herself. The good person will do the right actions, and can even die for his or her country. Dying for others is considered to be virtuous, in that it benefits others while achieving glory for the one who does this fine deed. This person can also sacrifice money and offices for his friends.

Student: Aristotle also analyzes a dispute about the happy person and whether he needs friends.

Teacher: That is correct, and the question touches on the issue of the goodness of friendship and how it can contribute to the life of someone who is already completely happy, and does not need friends for utility.

Aristotle ranks friendship as the greatest external good, as we have seen.

Student: An external good is something that is not within us?

Teacher: Yes, and usually an external good is something like wealth and honor. A good friend definitely seems to be something far superior to wealth and honor, but the question is whether a friend is a necessary good.

Student: A friend is someone we can benefit and with whom we can practice virtue.

Teacher: That is definitely one of the advantages of having friends. Aristotle also claims that, since we are political animals, it does not make sense to live alone. In addition, happiness is a kind of activity and observing others do good things is pleasant, especially if they are our friends, which means we can think of their actions as our own. Being alone affords fewer opportunities to be active and to be virtuous. Aristotle concludes that the happy person needs friends, indeed cannot be happy without friends.

Student: Aristotle also poses a question regarding the number of friends we should have.

Teacher: Yes, and Aristotle says that in friendship for pleasure or utility a small number of friends is the best option, although it is easier to have friends in these categories, but we should have as many good friends as possible.

Student: Aristotle also thinks of living together as a characteristic of friendship.

Teacher: That is true, but it consists in sharing conversation and thought more than anything else. Even so, these requirements do limit the number of people that we can be friends with. Consequently, close friendship is only possible with a few people. In addition, it is difficult to find many good people with whom we can be friends.

Student: Aristotle also states that it is good to have friends in all circumstances, in good and bad times.

Teacher: Yes, good friends are important in times of good and ill fortune. Friends are needed in ill fortune, but in good fortune we can help our friends. Sharing our distress with friends brings relief. At the same time, we do not wish to distress them with our ill fortune, and we do not wish to share bad things with them. Instead, we like to share our good fortune with them. Generally speaking, we should always be prepared to help our friends.

Student: Aristotle has a very complete conception of friendship.

Teacher: Absolutely. He distinguishes between three kinds of friendship, and favors the friendship based on virtue. He details what is required in friendship, such as spending time together. He has a broad conception of friendship in automatically considering siblings and spouses as friends, and he highlights the place of friendship in ethical theory, in establishing the connection between friendship and benevolence, and voluntariness.

Student: It is interesting how Aristotle treats friendship in general, in its connection with general questions pertaining to ethics, while at the same time paying attention to the particular circumstances of his society, and also more general aspects of human nature.

Teacher: I agree, and it is interesting to see how he distinguishes between young and older people when it comes to forming friendships. It still sounds very true today, as do many of his ethical views.

Student: Cicero also has a detailed treatment of friendship.

Teacher: Yes, and we have seen that he presents many of his predecessors' philosophical theories in his own words, and in a very personal style. In addition, he also thinks of philosophical theories as things that are meant to help us in practical ways, and not just as theories to be considered from a purely intellectual point of view.

Student: He was probably following the views of the Stoics and the Epicureans on the practical applications of philosophy.

Teacher: Most probably. His dialogue on friendship, titled *Laelius, on Friendship*, is based on a conversation he heard from one of his teachers regarding a discussion among several distinguished Romans.

Student: In this work, does he share Aristotle's views?

Teacher: He does, but he also gives practical advice. Aristotle examines particular puzzles and cases, concerning virtuous behavior, in his *Nicomachean Ethics*, which is also a practical way of looking at friendship. Cicero's approach is perhaps even more practical, and his analysis of friendship is based on the account of a particular friendship, the one which bound together Laelius and Scipio Africanus, who had died shortly before the reported dialogue.

Student: Laelius is speaking about a particular friendship, then?

Teacher: Yes, and both Laelius and Scipio were successfully involved in politics and were known for their virtues. While Cicero was conversant with Aristotle's theory of virtue, his approach is somewhat different. He thinks that true friendship is rare because it is difficult to find two truly good human beings, and true friendship has to be based on true virtue. In the dialogue, Laelius states that friendship is only possible between two good men.

Student: In this case, Laelius, according to Cicero, views friendship in a more specific way than does Aristotle.

Teacher: That is correct; he thinks of true friendship as existing between two exceptionally good men. Within Cicero's works, there is usually a political context, which is not surprising since he was himself a famous politician in Republican Rome.

In addition, if we accept that Laelius' description of friendship represents Cicero's own views, we can add that Cicero thinks of friendship as stronger than kinship, that is to say, than family ties.

Student: Do you think that Aristotle would agree with that?

Teacher: It is possible, because true friendship involves equality, and family relations are not truly between equals, except, perhaps, between siblings. Husband and wife are not equals, and neither are parents and children. Aristotle thinks of friendship as associated with politics and a political organization involves rulers and those who are ruled. For his part, Cicero focuses on the relationship between two virtuous men, who can be politicians, and they are his model and ideal for true friendship.

Student: For Laelius, in Cicero's dialogue, friendship necessarily involves goodwill.

Teacher: Yes, friends wish each other well and are affectionate towards each other. There must be an identity of feeling. Perhaps Laelius assumes that friends should have similar tastes.

Student: And for him friendship is superior to any external good.

Teacher: That is right, friendship is superior to wealth, power and public honors. It is compared with wisdom, and it rests on moral goodness. There is also frankness between friends, and they should be relaxed in each other's company.

Student: And according to Laelius, it is not possible to be happy without friendship.

Teacher: Exactly, and more to the point, life is not worth living without friendship. In this sense, Cicero believes that human nature is naturally sociable and that it is friendship or innate kindness that holds communities together. Friendship comes from natural affection.

Student: In that sense, friendship is something natural which explains our inclination to seek each other's company.

Teacher: Yes, and perhaps there is a similarity with Shaftesbury on this point, or perhaps Shaftesbury was inspired by Cicero, since Cicero's work was so well known. For Cicero, friendship is akin to love and it is natural feeling binding human beings. It is also observable in other species, in the way, for instance, that animals love their offspring. In addition, friendship does not arise out of some extraneous need, except for the company of one's friend. True friendship is not based on expediency or utility.

Student: According to this theory, we are attracted to the goodness of our friends.

Teacher: Correct, and in that sense Laelius or Cicero is adopting Aristotle's theory which states that we are attracted to the good. More specifically, the will aims at the good, as an inclination that has the good as its goal. In addition, Laelius says that we enjoy the company and the character of our friends. There is a clear association between friendship, wisdom and virtue.

Student: Laelius also thinks that friendship comes from nature.

Teacher: That is right, which means that it is something natural, and can obviously be developed. This position indicates that Cicero believes that human nature is, in principle, fundamentally good.

Student: In the dialogue, Laelius also mentions obstacles to friendship.

Teacher: Yes, if there is rivalry between the friends. This is particularly problematic in politics, when both friends are seeking high office. It is also difficult for a friendship to last beyond boyhood, if the characters of the friends evolve in different ways.

In addition, and as we have seen in Aristotle, the friendship can be broken if one of the friends asks the other to do something wrong.

Student: Laelius also mentions wrong opinions or approaches to friendship.

Teacher: Yes, Laelius thinks that those who prefer to keep a loose bond with friends are in the wrong, since trust is such an important element within friendship, and emotions are also important. Those defending that view do not wish to have any distress when things go wrong for our friends; however, emotional commitment is essential in friendship. Indeed, affection is what binds friends, and what we need from our friends. Admiration for one another is also a central part of friendship.

He also rejects the view stating that the goal of friendship is utility.

Student: The question of equality between friends is also mentioned by Laelius.

Teacher: This is an interesting aspect of the dialogue. Equality is important in friendship, but at the same time it is fine to love our friends more than ourselves; there is no restriction in that sense. According to Laelius, we can treat them better than we treat ourselves, and we can even love them more than they love themselves.

Student: Is it clear that Laelius believes that one should not hold back in our love and admiration for our friends?

Teacher: That is one of the main ideas put forward in Cicero's dialogue on friendship, and it is certainly commendable if, as friends, we give more than we receive.

Student: That view would be in line with Aristotle's general rule to the effect that it is better to be active than passive, and in that sense, it is better to give than to receive.

Does Laelius describe other aspects of a solid friendship?

Teacher: He states that we should not enjoy hearing criticism of our friends.

Student: That makes sense, since there is a unity of affection between friends. Perhaps, if we enjoy hearing criticism of our friends, it could mean that we bear some grudge against them, or that we are not as supportive of them as we should be.

Teacher: At the same time, we should not assume that we have been slighted by our friends, which could indicate a lack of trust in them. If our friends have done something wrong, we should gently correct them, and we should generally advise them well. Sincerity is a very important aspect and flattery should have no place in a friendship.

In addition, there should be no hypocrisy or pretense, and at the same time we should be pleasant with our friends, and not formal. We should not expect our friends to be something that they are not, or better than they are. In that sense, it is better to have friends like us.

Student: Laelius also addresses the question whether it is better to have new or old friends.

Teacher: He does address that question and prefers older friendships, although new ones should not be avoided. One should be open to making new friendships. In addition, we tend to enjoy friends who are our own age more.

Student: That makes sense, since they will probably have more in common with us.

Laelius also states that pleasures should be enjoyed in company.

Teacher: That is right, and this is similar to Shaftesbury's position. Whatever pleasures we can enjoy, they are enhanced by the company of friends, or other human beings, generally speaking.

Student: Laelius does take into account the possibility that a friendship could be dissolved, does he not?

Teacher: Yes; however, he states that the friendship should never turn into hostility, and he also says that it is better not to turn friends into enemies. In addition, one should not end the friendship abruptly.

In general, for Laelius, and Cicero, friendship is similar to virtue and wisdom, and it accompanies virtue and wisdom, and it is in that way one of the greatest goods available to us.

Student: What else can we say about friendship that perhaps was not mentioned explicitly?

Teacher: We could expand on the connection between friendship and the virtues and the way in which friendship is a way of exercising virtues. We can be brave for our friends, while justice is subsumed under friendship. Giving to friends is also important, and generally being generous towards our friends. We should tell the truth, and be friendly as well as witty in the company of our friends. We can be advised by our friends and benefit from their knowledge and wisdom.

Student: Perhaps there is a theoretical as well as a practical aspect to friendship?

Teacher: That is right. On the one hand, there is the emotional aspect, which is very important. The emotional bond cannot be ignored and it is a sure foundation for friendship. It means that we share joys and sorrows with our friends.

There is also the theoretical aspect, in the sense that we have similar intellectual interests with our friends, and can share our knowledge with them, and benefit from their knowledge and wisdom. This is certainly also a very important aspect, the ability to learn from our friends' experience and their studies. This theoretical aspect is also very important. Shaftesbury states that even intellectual pursuits are best enjoyed in company. Perhaps we could add that friends are precious sources of knowledge given their life experience and theoretical studies.

Student: It does seem that friendship is something that goes over and above normal moral duties and even virtue. We are expected to help others and generally to be just and fair towards them. However, we are not obliged to have friends.

Teacher: Precisely. We live in community and depend on others for our physical and intellectual needs. But friendship seems to be something over and above the provision of those basic needs. It reflects our social nature and a certain bond that is moral and profoundly human. It is based on empathy but goes beyond that and develops into a moral activity. Our desire to have friends shows the kind of natural affection which Shaftesbury considers to be typically human. True friendship is based not on utilitarian concerns but on a natural kind of sociability which is based on human nature while providing the means to perfect that human nature.

Student: It seems that friendship is a kind of super-virtue, in the sense that it includes the other virtues and goes beyond virtue as something that is expected of us.

Teacher: I agree.

Student: It seems that Aristotle and Cicero privilege friendship with those who are similar to us.

Teacher: Aristotle also contemplates friendship between husband and wife, parents and children, and Cicero states that the friends may come from different social backgrounds. However, they seem to have in mind, as perfect friends, two virtuous adult males.

Student: I understand. But if the possibility of learning from our friends is important, then it is also good to have friends from different backgrounds.

Teacher: Yes, and in that way we can also learn more about ourselves, which is another great benefit of having friends.

Student: Perhaps the contemporary views on friendship emphasize the subjective aspects on friendship, like sharing personal tastes in music or literature, or other activities, instead of focusing on moral issues and the role of friendship within society.

Teacher: That is why it is important to remind ourselves of Aristotle's and Cicero's views. Even if we think of friendship as a matter of individual and personal tastes, as something private, a phenomenon that is commented on by Alasdair MacIntyre, the moral aspect is always present. Can we really be friends with someone we do not admire, or someone whom we consider to do the kinds of things that are morally objectionable? Perhaps we can get along in some cases, but it would not be true friendship. There is always a moral element to friendship.

Student: As a general issue that affects friendship, is it not a problem that we favor one person over others? Would it not be preferable to be friends with everyone or at least friendly to everyone?

Teacher: Friendship is based on mutual interests, and on being good and virtuous. In theory we could be friends with any one who is good. However, this would not be possible from a practical point of view, as we have seen. We only have limited time to be with friends, because we have numerous activities. In addition, it is impossible to meet everyone who is potentially a good friend. Instead we meet our friends due to particular circumstances that make us cross paths.

Student: But we can be good to everyone we encounter.

Teacher: Certainly, we could and should be good to the people we encounter. But a close kind of friendship is limited to a few people. In addition to the requirement of being virtuous, it is also important to have similar interests, since an important part of friendship consists in spending time together and sharing certain activities.

In that sense, too, we must help those around us, because it is easier and more practical than helping those who are far from us.

5.4. The Intellectual Virtues

Student: Aristotle also considers the existence of intellectual virtues. However, one tends to think of virtue as something practical rather than theoretical.

Teacher: That is right, and naturally the intellectual virtues have their focus on reason more than the will or the practical intellect. Nevertheless, we have seen that virtue always requires the use of reason and that it entails a coordination between the will and reason. Even among the cardinal virtues, as they came to be known, one was considered to be more theoretical than the others, namely, wisdom or prudence. Indeed, prudence is considered to be among the intellectual virtues.

Student: These virtues also have several things in common with the moral virtues.

Teacher: Yes, and Aristotle assigns the intellectual virtues to the theoretical part of the soul, as opposed to the practical or that part which rationally calculates or deliberates. The moral and the intellectual virtues are different but they are also linked in the way that decision requires thought, or the activity of the theoretical part of the soul. Aristotle states that by itself, thought does not produce anything, so it must be combined with desire in order to turn into action. Deliberation concerns things that can be changed, and not those that have already happened and are in the past. Virtues of thought are all concerned with the truth.

Student: And there are somewhat different ways of grasping the truth.

Teacher: Yes, and Aristotle states that they are craft, scientific knowledge ('epistēmē'), prudence or practical wisdom ('phronēsis'), wisdom or theoretical wisdom ('sophia'), and understanding ('nous'). He goes on to explain each of these intellectual virtues in detail.

Science or scientific knowledge concerns that which does not change. Aristotle assumes that what changes cannot be known for certain when it cannot be observed. The object of science is therefore what is necessary and eternal, since Aristotle understands the necessary as that which cannot be otherwise and is everlasting.

Student: If science pertains to that which is necessary and everlasting, then does it have a restricted scope?

Teacher: Yes, in principle, it would be limited to the heavenly spheres, and obviously the Prime Mover. However, Aristotle does not seem to exclude completely knowledge of that which changes.

Student: In addition to the view that science concerns what does not change, it seems that science itself should not change.

Teacher: I agree on that point; true knowledge should not change. Another characteristic of science is that it can be taught and it can be learned.

Student: In the *Nicomachean Ethics*, Aristotle mentions theoretical knowledge or science as a virtue, but he also mentions it in other works, in a somewhat different way.

Teacher: Yes, and at this point, he makes a reference to the *Analytics*, in a clear reference to the *Posterior Analytics*, which is Aristotle's main work on the theory of knowledge.

Student: Is there a difference between the two approaches to science or scientific knowledge? In what sense is knowledge a virtue?

Teacher: There are many points in common between Aristotle's treatment of scientific knowledge in *Posterior Analytics*, which contains a much more detailed treatment of scientific knowledge, and in the *Nicomachean Ethics*. In the latter, he also mentions induction and deduction, as describing the process of acquiring knowledge, respectively starting with particulars or starting with universals. In the *Nicomachean Ethics*, he mentions teaching through induction and deduction. He explicitly states that this is the same kind of knowledge that is described in the *Posterior Analytics*, and it implies knowing principles better than the conclusion. It is therefore demonstrative knowledge, or knowledge of the universal, as opposed to perceiving individual things.

Student: Perhaps scientific knowledge has a practical outcome in the *Nicomachean Ethics*?

Teacher: Aristotle does not mention the practical application of scientific knowledge in this section, but since this work is about practical philosophy, one would be justified in establishing that kind of link. In that sense, scientific knowledge as virtue ought to imply the putting into practice of this knowledge and recalling it often, as well as practicing those things that produce this kind of knowledge. One may assume that knowledge of metaphysical issues, for instance, the nature of God, can lead to a better practice of piety, and the two virtues can thus be linked.

Student: Aristotle also considers craft knowledge as an intellectual virtue, does he not?

Teacher: He does, and he recalls two different kinds of activity, which can lead or not lead to a product, as production and action, respectively. Craft knowledge implies production. Naturally, this kind of knowledge leads to practice, and it consists in the knowledge that leads to production, as reason applied to production. With regard to this knowledge, Aristotle explicitly distinguishes it from knowledge of that which is necessary, since a product can change, and also from knowledge of that which is natural and comes to be or develops by itself.

Student: Would one be expected to have these virtues in the same way as the moral virtues?

Teacher: We have seen that, ideally, one should have all the moral virtues. With regard to scientific knowledge, it may help one to become more virtuous. As for craft, it is perhaps not immediately clear that one becomes morally better by mastering a craft. However, craft clearly entails the combination of knowledge and practice, and in that sense, it is akin to the other virtues.

Student: Aristotle then describes prudence, which has a prominent place among the intellectual virtues.

Teacher: This is a central virtue, for Plato, Aristotle, and later philosophers, like Aquinas. For Aristotle, it is an intellectual virtue, but it is clearly directed at practical matters and its goal is human happiness. On the one hand, it concerns the choice of the means in a given action, but it also concerns the end of the action broadly speaking.

Student: Does it mean what we usually mean by prudence?

Teacher: It means more than that and, in that sense, it is a much broader term, like wisdom, or more specifically practical wisdom. It does not mean primarily caution but a thoughtful management of one's affairs and deliberation on moral conduct. In a certain way, it can be considered as complete practical virtue, since it also concerns particular action and knowing particular circumstances, but it indicates a strong deliberative and also theoretical content.

Student: It is a preeminent virtue, then, and those who possess it can be considered virtuous?

Teacher: Absolutely, and Aristotle states that we learn about this virtue by learning about the prudent person. It implies deliberation about what is good and beneficial in general for human life. In that sense, it is a general virtue in principle, but it is applied to particular cases.

Student: There seems to be some ambiguity as to whether it concerns particulars or universals, and therefore whether it is more practical or theoretical.

Teacher: That is because it is a very complete virtue. However, we have seen that other virtues have a claim to being complete virtues, such as justice. One sign that it is practical is that it concerns things or states of affairs that can be changed. In that sense, it differs from scientific knowledge and demonstration. It is also not knowledge of a craft because it is about action rather than production.

Student: How does Aristotle define prudence, then?

Teacher: He conceives it as a state which includes awareness of the truth, it includes reason, and it is applied to action concerning that which is good or bad for us as human beings. As a prudent person, Aristotle gives the example of Pericles and mentions also politicians and those who run households as exemplars of prudence. He establishes a link between temperance and prudence in the sense that temperance preserves prudence. This is based on the assumption that our decisions about actions can be hampered if our inclinations, and questions of pleasure and pain, are not controlled by reason through temperance.

Student: Prudence seems to be a broad intellectual virtue.

Teacher: That is right; it concerns general deliberation about action, and that which can be otherwise. In that sense it is a very complete virtue. Aristotle also mentions different types of prudence, such as political prudence, which is employed in managing the political state and legislating, and it belongs to the political class. Aristotle associates this type of prudence with political science.

Student: Aristotle mentions several types of prudence in this context.

Teacher: Yes, within political prudence he distinguishes legislative prudence and deliberative prudence within a political context, which are required for legislating and decreeing, as the more theoretical and practical sides of political prudence, respectively. He also considers household science as prudence. He seems to consider political prudence as public prudence, but he also distinguishes political from legislative prudence, perhaps thinking here of political prudence as more practical, and divides political prudence into deliberative and judicial.

Student: It seems that Aristotle thinks of prudence as having an application within the city and the household and also individually by each person.

Teacher: Yes, and he assumes that the kind of prudence employed by an individual is the typical kind of prudence. However, he states that prudence applied to the family or the body politic is also an important aspect of prudence.

Student: Does he also makes distinctions regarding age in this context?

Teacher: He argues that prudence is more readily found among older people, rather than young people, because prudence concerns particulars, which are known by experience, and older people have more experience. For that reason, too, younger people are particularly good at mathematics, which is an abstract and universal field of knowledge. In this sense, prudence is opposed to understanding by dealing essentially with particulars.

Student: Aristotle also discusses understanding, or intellectual knowledge ('nous').

Teacher: Yes, and understanding regards more properly the principles, while scientific knowledge is about the demonstrations which follow from those principles. Craft knowledge and prudence differ from scientific knowledge and understanding, since they concern things that can be otherwise. In turn, wisdom ('sophia') can be associated with craft knowledge, but it is more closely related to theoretical knowledge.

Student: In that sense, a craftsman can be wise?

Teacher: That is what Aristotle states, but for him wisdom is complete knowledge, embracing scientific knowledge and understanding.

Student: Does Aristotle make a distinction between theoretical and practical aspects of these virtues at this stage?

Teacher: In the section devoted to the intellectual virtues, in the *Nicomachean Ethics*, Aristotle thinks of craft knowledge and prudence as having immediate practical applications, while scientific knowledge, understanding and wisdom have a more theoretical aspect. He considers wisdom the greatest virtue because it concerns the most important things, and not just practical issues that pertain to human living. Human circumstances can change from place to place, but the content of wisdom does not change.

Student: We return to the difference between universal and particular, and Aristotle's preference for universal knowledge.

Teacher: I agree, and prudence can also concern universal principles, but it cannot disregard particular cases; indeed, it is more centered on particulars. Moreover, wisdom is knowledge of the best, divinelike principle, which is very important because Aristotle holds that human beings are not the most perfect beings in the universe, and wisdom contemplates the most perfect beings.

Student: Aristotle also mentions deliberation again in this context.

Teacher: This is an important aspect which goes hand in hand with prudence. We have seen that prudence involves the grasp of the truth but that it also concerns universals and particulars, thus straddling the intellectual and the moral virtues. Deliberation concerns what is best for us as human beings and also the means to achieve the desired end. It involves inquiry and the use of reasoning, and it does not tend to be a quick process. It concerns, naturally, that which is not previously determined. Obviously, it does not concern that which is eternal and immutable, but that which can be changed. There is good and bad deliberation, the former involving the correct means or way to reach the truth or the desired outcome, which is the right thing to do. Its goodness also depends on the good quality of the end.

Student: It makes sense for Aristotle to define deliberation in connection with the intellectual virtues, given its close link with prudence.

Teacher: Yes, and comprehension (gnomē) is also associated with deliberation, and it judges while prudence prescribes. It means to understand something pertaining to prudence but it does not presuppose having prudence. Those who have prudence and understanding also tend to have comprehension and considerateness, which judges what is true. Understanding in this context also studies particulars and goes hand in hand with the other operations of the intellect mentioned in this debate.

Student: Aristotle also speculates on the practical applications of prudence and wisdom.

Teacher: That is correct, and the question is whether they have an immediate application. He asks, for instance, whether we could simply benefit from a prudent person's good advice, in the same way that we consult physicians in order to stay healthy.

Student: I can understand that, since having theoretical knowledge does not always lead to its application. At the same time, the purpose of this kind of knowledge should be practical.

Teacher: Aristotle states that wisdom and prudence are good in themselves regardless of whether they are applied, since they perfect the rational parts of the soul, theoretical and practical. Aristotle argues that wisdom by itself, as a state, makes us happy. By wisdom and prudence the goal is correct; they make us choose the right goal. However, to be virtuous we should aim at the right goal for the right reasons, and not reluctantly or simply because we are somehow obliged by the laws, for instance. He mentions cleverness as the ability which allows us to reach the goal, but it is only allied with prudence if the goal is good.

Student: In concluding the discussion of the intellectual virtues in the *Nicomachean Ethics*, Aristotle also talks about complete virtue.

Teacher: That is right. He says that there is natural virtue, but it requires development. He also suggests that some of us naturally have particular virtues. The virtues also require reflection and, in that way, they must be consciously developed. Virtue must develop beyond its natural state, and that requires understanding, and complete virtue requires prudence. He mentions Socrates and his high opinion of prudence. For Aristotle, not all virtue is prudence but it requires prudence. It must accord with and follow correct reason, which is in line with prudence. To be virtuous means to be aligned with prudence.

Student: Aristotle also tackles the issues of the unity of the virtues.

Teacher: Absolutely; he thinks of prudence as this single state involving all the virtues. To be good we need prudence, and prudence is underpinned by virtue of character. If one only has natural virtue, it is possible to have one virtue and not the other virtues, but complete virtue must include prudence.

Student: He also explains the connection between virtue, broadly speaking, and prudence.

Teacher: Exactly, and virtue is needed in order to choose the right goal, while prudence is needed to choose the means to achieving that goal. In that sense, they are inseparable. And virtue and prudence perfect the soul, which leads to happiness. Nevertheless, Aristotle thinks of wisdom as having a higher object than prudence, as we have seen.

Student: Aquinas also mentions the importance of the intellectual virtues, does he not?

Teacher: Yes, he thinks of prudence as inhering in reason while having as its principle the rectitude of the will.

Student: Does he clearly distinguish prudence from science?

Teacher: Yes, while prudence is right reason about things to be done, science ('scientia') is right reason about speculative truths. He states that the acts of the intellectual virtues can be meritorious, and they consist in contemplation of the truth, which leads to perfect happiness.

Student: Does Aquinas explain in what way the intellectual virtues can be described as virtues?

Teacher: He states that they are habits of the speculative intellect, and they lead to the good work of the intellect. For him, wisdom ('sapientia') considers the highest causes. He considers wisdom to be more perfect than science in the sense that it judges of all sciences regarding both their principles and conclusions.

Student: He thus believes in a hierarchy of the intellectual virtues?

Teacher: Yes, he states that science depends on understanding or intellect, and they both depend on wisdom. By these intellectual virtues and habits, we know and tell the truth, which is above opinion. This corresponds to Aristotle's conception of wisdom as being more complete than both understanding, which deals with principles, and science, which infers the conclusions from the principles. In addition, he argues that according to Aristotle, art or craft is not a speculative or intellectual virtue but has something in common with them in that they produce the ability to work well, although they do not involve the control or perfection of the appetite.

Student: There is something else needed in order to use art or craft well, is there not?

Teacher: Yes, that is a very important point. According to Aquinas in the *Summa Theologiae*, a good will is necessary to make good use of art, and that good will is perfected by virtue. It is moral virtue that can lead to the good use of art. He also expands on the similarity between the arts and the intellectual virtues, in the way that making a syllogism can be considered an art or craft, as well as making a speech and counting or measuring.

Student: Aquinas also mentions the liberal arts in this context.

Teacher: Precisely, and the liberal arts developed in late Antiquity and during the Middle Ages. They are based on the use of numbers and words, like arithmetic and music, on the one hand, or grammar, on the other. Aquinas explains that they do not involve the work of the body and therefore are considered to entail freedom. In the context of the discussion of the intellectual virtues, he states that prudence confers not only aptness for good work but also the use of good work.

Student: It seems that for Aquinas prudence stands midway between the moral and the intellectual virtues.

Teacher: Yes, but as for Aristotle, he classes it under the intellectual virtues. Prudence is a virtue that perfects reason and directs it to the means to the right end. As we have seen, memory, understanding and foresight are parts of prudence, as well as caution, for instance.

Student: And in general, Aquinas states that virtue is based on reason, right?

Teacher: Yes, virtue is the perfection of human nature in its specificity, and reason is something that is specifically human, therefore virtue involves the use of reason. If reason commands the appetitive faculty, then moral virtue happens in so far as the appetitive faculty obeys reason.

Student: And Aquinas also makes the connection between the moral and the intellectual virtues?

Teacher: He accepts the view that moral virtue is typically considered true virtue. However, for someone to do a good deed, reason must be disposed through a habit of intellectual virtue and, in addition, the appetite must be well disposed through the habit of moral virtue, as he states in the *Summa Theologiae*. Moral virtue is primarily about the appetite, and the way that it follows reason, and intellectual virtue is about reason. Moral habits should conform to reason. An intellectual virtue perfects the intellect, theoretical or practical, while moral virtue perfects one's appetite.

Student: And the will is rational appetite for Aquinas, then?

Teacher: Yes, as opposed to appetite, broadly speaking. The will is right when it follows the truth, which is perceived by the intellect. And therefore the will is involved in moral action.

Prudence belongs in the conception of moral virtue in the sense that all moral virtues come under the umbrella of prudence in receiving its guidance. Prudence shows the link between moral and intellectual virtues, because moral action requires prudence. It also requires understanding, although it does not require wisdom, science or art.

Student: Are there other aspects of prudence which indicate that it is an intellectual virtue?

Teacher: Aquinas states that in choosing an action, if we consider the end and the means to the end, then the right end is chosen through moral virtue, and the intention is good in this way, by inclining the appetitive faculty to a good which conforms with reason. The means is subsequently chosen through prudence, through counsel, judgment and command, in this order. Understanding is needed because the knowledge of first principles is also essential for theoretical and practical matters, and in this sense, understanding is associated with the theoretical intellect, and prudence with the practical intellect. Understanding is about right reason in theoretical matters, while prudence consists in right reason concerning that which is to be done.

Student: Naturally, Aquinas assumes that choice entails the use of reason?

Teacher: Exactly. We have a natural inclination, which does not involve reason, but choice involves reason and it must be perfected by intellectual virtue.

Student: It is clear that the moral virtues require prudence and understanding, which are intellectual virtues. Do the intellectual virtues require the moral virtues?

Teacher: Among the intellectual virtues, it is prudence which requires moral virtue. It reasons about universal and particular principles. It can obtain universal principles from the understanding, such as the principle to do no evil. For the particular ends, the experience resulting from the moral virtues is essential, as well as the habits which perfect those moral virtues. Aquinas explains that vice may result from knowing the universal principles but not applying them in particular cases; alternatively, they may be destroyed by a passion. In order for someone to be predisposed to particular principles of action, the moral virtues are required, as well as a certain knowledge.

Student: Does Aquinas explain whether reason or the appetite strives for the end?

Teacher: Reason apprehends the end, and therefore it comes first in thinking about moral action. However, in arguing about the choice of means, which is effected by prudence, the appetite precedes reason.

Student: It does seem that reason comes first.

Teacher: It does, in absolute terms, and therefore Aquinas is a rationalist when it comes to moral action, because rather than placing the focus on the will, as later philosophers would do, he stresses the role of reason. In the *Summa Theologica*, he states that the good of moral virtue consists in following reason. Voluntarist philosophers went on to favor the role of the will over the intellect.

Student: I understand how moral and intellectual virtues are interrelated. Are there other ways in which prudence helps the moral virtues?

Teacher: Prudence, in directing counsel, judgment and command, removes the impediment of the passions, which are movements of the sensitive appetite, and which are inimical to moral action.

Student: And are intellectual virtues also related among themselves?

Teacher: According to Aquinas, the different sciences and arts have different subject matters, and in that sense, they are not as closely related among themselves as the moral virtues, as we have seen in discussing the general distinction between moral and intellectual virtues. Prudence ensures that the moral virtues, which are about passions and operations, are unified. All passions go back to love and hatred and terminate in pleasure and sorrow.

Student: We have seen that for Aquinas, the cardinal virtues comprise both intellectual and moral virtues.

Teacher: Yes, and for Aquinas, rectitude of the appetite underpins the perfect idea of virtue. Perfect virtue gives the capacity for doing well and produces the good deed. Equally, the cardinal virtues imply rectitude of the appetite.

Student: We have seen that the theological virtues have God as their object and they are infused by God. Does Aquinas state whether God has virtues?

Teacher: That is a good question, because the virtues are associated with the soul and God does not have a soul in the sense of having that which manages the body, for God does not have a body. However, God has an intellect and that is where we can find an analogy with human virtue.

Student: It is also clear that Jesus has the virtues.

Teacher: Yes, and Jesus is the perfect exemplar of virtue, according to Aquinas. However, he speaks of virtue in God also in a more general way. Inspired by Augustine, he states that in the same way that the types or forms of all things pre-exist in God, the same must happen with virtue. Justice exists originally in God. In this sense, Aquinas identifies the exemplar virtues with divine virtue. Prudence is the divine mind, and temperance consists in God's self-contemplation. God's unchangeableness is his courage, and divine justice is his observance of the eternal law, established by himself.

Student: And the cardinal virtues in us can also be directed to God.

Teacher: That is right. Prudence in that sense consists in contemplating that which pertains to God, and disregarding the things of the world. Temperance disregards the needs of the body, while courage ensures that we are not afraid of neglecting the body. Justice ensures that this is the path followed by the soul. These are the perfecting virtues, and Aquinas also mentions the perfect virtues, which are the completion of the perfecting virtues. In that sense, prudence only knows the things of God, temperance does not know earthly desires, courage does not know passion and justice allows the union with the divine mind.

Student: It seems that those would be the typical virtues of a religious person.

Teacher: They do seem like the typical virtues practiced by someone in a religious order, although not necessarily because they are to be found only in a religious order. These virtues surpass the passions. Aquinas follows Plotinus in describing these virtues, with this particular classification, as social virtues, which are the human virtues, followed by the perfecting and the perfect virtues, which are about the divine and represent a higher control of the passions or a complete disregard for the passions. Above those are the exemplar virtues, belonging to God.

5.5. Vice

Student: It would appear that vice is the opposite of virtue.

Teacher: Yes, although it can indicate not just lack of virtue but a conscious choice of evil actions. Vice can include the omission of virtue or the active pursuit of vicious inclinations.

In addition, in the *Summa Theologica*, Aquinas quotes Augustine to the effect that every virtue has opposing vices, and some vices represent a semblance of the virtues.

Student: If virtue requires taking into account the circumstances, as well as the capabilities of the subject while considering the object of the action, then it must be easy to fail to be virtuous.

Teacher: Virtue definitely requires an effort as well as the use of reason, and in that sense, it entails a complex process. Everyone is expected to be virtuous in certain circumstances, even if the perfectly virtuous person tends to be rare. In the *Politics*, Aristotle considers the possibility that some human beings may never be educated to become virtuous. One should not be considered vicious if one fails to act virtuously in certain cases. Aristotle is particularly concerned with intemperance and incontinence.

Student: Perhaps we could look first into the question of vice and sin in general, before discussing details. Aquinas speaks specifically of sin and vice as the opposite of virtue.

Teacher: Aquinas thinks of malice, sin and vice as the opposites of virtue. Vice is the general opposite, while sin implies specific actions. Malice indicates specifically the opposition to virtue as goodness, and in that sense, it seems to indicate a deliberate choice of evil. Nowadays, we tend to think of sin as a term with religious connotations, but Aquinas does not think of sin as opposed to vice in that way, but appears to think of the distinction as being a question of more general or more specific principles.

Student: Does Aquinas give specific reasons for the existence of vice in us?

Teacher: He puts it down to a deviation from reason, and following our sensitive nature rather than reason. He also accepts Aristotle's view that for achieving virtuous actions many elements are required, while evil can result from one single defect. Aquinas also states that sin is an act of the will.

Student: Is sin then something that is always deliberate?

Teacher: There are sins which come down to neglecting to do the right thing, but Aquinas holds that sin is always voluntary. It is in our power to will and not to will, and not willing the right thing, in that sense, is a voluntary action. He also states that sin is about desiring something or avoiding something in an inordinate way. This comes down to self-love which makes us desire certain things and avoid others.

Student: I understand how self-love can lead us to neglect virtue. Are there other reasons for committing sins?

Teacher: Sin also arises from ignorance, and a defect in reason or the impulse of the sensitive appetite.

Student: It seems that vice implies that the will does not follow right reason?

Teacher: Yes, all these elements are involved, the will, reason and also the sensitive appetite. The will should follow right reason, and the sensitive appetite should conform to the decision of the will by observing right reason. With regard to the virtues, there can be specific vices pertaining to the lack of specific virtues. A good example is the extremes between which each virtue is situated. In that sense, in the case of courage, for instance, being foolhardy or a coward are both vices.

Student: Is vice always a question of missing the mean?

Teacher: In his *Commentary on the* Nicomachean Ethics, Aquinas states that vice is not just a question of missing the mean. Some actions are evil by their own nature, like homicide and adultery.

Student: Aristotle also delves into the question of temperance, intemperance and incontinence.

Teacher: This was a problem that puzzled philosophers, namely the role of reason and the will in human action. Socrates defended the position that one only does evil out of ignorance. However, Aristotle recognizes that we can do evil when knowing the truth and the right thing to do, but not wishing to adhere to it.

Student: It seems that the problem lies in the interaction between knowledge and the emotions, and therefore the interaction between the different parts of the soul.

Teacher: That is correct, because Aristotle thinks that the emotions are an integral part of being human, and play an important role in human conduct, and can be useful in that way. He does not think that vice comes down only to ignorance. The emotions do not involve primarily the intellect, and so this is a question also of the lower faculties of the soul, and not just the intellect.

Student: He makes a distinction between the temperate person and the continent person.

Teacher: Yes, and the temperate person is, obviously, virtuous, since temperance is a virtue and the temperate person acts in accordance with temperance.

Student: This is not about just any kind of vice, is it?

Teacher: In this context, Aristotle studies the cases when someone is not virtuous in the matter of pleasures and pains, and this concerns the virtue of temperance or the vice of intemperance.

Student: Is there a particular reason why he focuses on this particular virtue and this particular vice?

Teacher: This is perhaps because Socrates had also mentioned this problem, as we observe it in the Platonic dialogues. However, in principle, the ignorance of any virtue leads to vice, according to Socrates in Plato's dialogues. In addition, it could be that other kinds of vices issue from intemperance or incontinence. One may become a coward, for instance, and lack the virtue of courage, by way of trying to avoid pain.

Student: I understand that Aristotle highlights here the significance of temperance. He distinguishes temperance and continence, as well as intemperance and incontinence.

Teacher: Yes. The temperate person is someone who has the correct appetite and follows right reason, while the continent person may have base appetites but follows reason. The temperate person does not have to fight his or her appetites.

Student: One might think of the continent person as more praiseworthy, since fighting one's appetites requires more effort.

Teacher: It might appear to be so. However, since virtue is a question of practice and acquiring good habits, the preparation for acquiring the right appetites, through habitual practice, is part of the process of becoming virtuous. In that sense, the continent person has a longer way to go in order to become virtuous.

Student: It seems that temperance does not only consist in having the knowledge, but in the control of the appetites.

Teacher: That is correct, and Aristotle even speaks of people acting on their beliefs which may not be exact knowledge, with regard to moral issues, but the important thing is the interrelation between knowledge and the application of that knowledge.

Student: And what is the difference between the incontinent and the intemperate person?

Teacher: The incontinent person knows the right thing to do but does not control himself or herself, while the intemperate person consciously chooses to commit excesses in the matter of pursuing pleasures and avoiding pains. Sometimes this happens even without an intense appetite motivating the action. Aristotle states that this is worse than following one's appetites, because if one commits an evil deed solely based on reason, then if a base appetite were added, the crime would be even more serious. In the same way, committing a crime intentionally is worse than committing it on the spur of the moment.

Student: It seems that, for Aristotle, feeling and appetite create major distinctions in the matter of vice.

Teacher: Yes, and Aristotle thinks that being moved by appetite or feeling is more natural and pardonable. Someone who is intemperate seems less prone to regret and to being cured.

Student: He also points to a distinction between vice, incontinence, and intemperance.

Teacher: Yes, vice being a more deep-seated trait, while incontinence is a temporary condition. The vicious person is less likely to accept his or her condition, while the incontinent person knows that he or she is incontinent. The intemperate person holds that it is right to pursue physical pleasure regardless of the moral consequences.

Student: It means that there is a problem of principles in the case of the intemperate person?

Teacher: Yes, and in the case of the incontinent person, it is a question of putting into practice the correct principles which the incontinent person already knows.

Student: Insofar as, for Aristotle and Aquinas, as well as other philosophers, virtue is very much about controlling and harnessing the passions, it makes sense to think of vice from the point of view of intemperance and incontinence.

Conclusion

Teacher: We have analyzed the main features of virtue ethics according to classical accounts, particularly those of Aristotle, Aquinas and Shaftesbury. We have decided to focus on these three authors because the literature on virtue ethics is so immensely vast. Virtue ethics remained the dominant approach to ethics in medieval philosophy, and this is a very long period in the history of philosophy, with many philosophers, Jewish, Christian, and Muslim, developing theories of virtue ethics.

Student: Yes, and it was important to first situate virtue ethics within the broader field of ethics. After our discussion, it becomes clear that virtue is an essential part of ethics and that the other kinds of normative ethics, such as ethics of duty and consequentialism, do not constitute a replacement for virtue ethics.

Teacher: Virtue never really went out of fashion and it is difficult to imagine the possibility of correct moral action from the point of view of the individual without a strong emphasis on virtue ethics. We have seen that there is no dichotomy between virtuous behavior and following the laws, in the sense that there is no tension between an emphasis on virtue and the principle of duty and the laws. This is made clear by Aristotle and Aquinas. Virtue and the laws, natural or positive, complement each other.

Student: It was also important, in the course of our discussion, to go through the principles of ethics, and its presuppositions.

Teacher: Yes, and some of these points are treated by Aristotle in a systematic way, setting the tone for centuries and millennia to come. The question of voluntary action, with all that it entails, is central to an understanding of ethics and its presuppositions. The principle of freedom is also very important.

Student: We have seen that voluntary action is not done by force, and that it requires awareness or knowledge, in the sense of not being done in ignorance. It involves decision and the outcome aimed at concerns what is good or bad; in other words, it concerns moral values. It also entails a wish for the end and deliberation about the means.

And these presuppositions are also part of virtue ethics. Virtue, like ethical conduct generally, implies dealing with others and treating them in the best possible way. Virtue is also about the development of character.

Teacher: We have also analyzed important aspects pertaining to ethics, such as the question of human nature.

Student: Naturally, the way we think of human nature is bound to influence the ethical theories that we develop and adopt. If we think that emotions are a natural part of human nature, as Aristotle did, then they have to be integrated into any virtue ethical theory.

Teacher: Precisely. Philosophers who prefer to focus on the rational aspect of human life, such as the Stoics and Spinoza, develop views on ethics which are more exclusively rational.

Student: The link between virtue and the soul is also essential to ancient, medieval and modern philosophers.

Teacher: I believe that that connection also holds today. Some philosophers may prefer to speak of mind instead of soul, but even so virtue certainly has a spiritual character and issues from other spiritual notions, such as freedom.

Student: Speaking of important notions, including spiritual notions, associated with ethics and virtue, the concept of good is an essential topic within this discussion.

Teacher: Absolutely. The good can be understood in many ways, as a form or a universal, or as a transcendental, but it is a spiritual entity which is central to ethics and also to virtue ethics. It is the goal of the will. As a human good, it is equated with happiness.

Student: We have seen that according to Aristotle, the good can be the ultimate goal, or a means to an end, in which case it would be identified with the useful.

It is interesting to see how philosophers discuss the themes of the good, virtue and happiness. It is especially interesting to study the connection between virtue and happiness.

Teacher: I agree. It seems that for the philosophers we have studied, virtue and happiness are the same, or very similar. At any rate, it is not possible to be happy without being virtuous, according to the philosophers we have studied.

Student: The Stoics say that virtue is the highest good, and that it suffices for happiness.

Teacher: That is right, although a philosopher like Aristotle would think of other goods as being necessary for happiness, external goods such as friends, and at least a moderate amount of wealth. However, he would agree that it is impossible to be happy without being virtuous, given the mental imbalance represented by vice. With regard to happiness itself, philosophers tend to agree that it is an ultimate goal, and not the means to an end. We do not wish to be happy for the sake of some other goal.

Student: And it is clear that for Aristotle and for other philosophers that we have studied, virtue consists in the perfection of human nature.

Teacher: That is undoubtedly the case. From both a theoretical and a practical perspective, virtue constitutes the culmination of human perfection.

Pleasure is also a topic that is discussed by Aristotle in the *Nicomachean Ethics* and in the *Eudemian Ethics*, as a kind of good and as something associated with happiness. Aristotle defends the notion that mental pleasures are the most important ones. This position would also be adopted by Aquinas and, in modern times, Shaftesbury.

Student: Pleasure is certainly an important topic in this context, since it is a principle that can move to action.

The various definitions of virtue offered by philosophers are very important and inspiring.

Teacher: Absolutely, and we can find some variations from ancient to medieval and modern philosophy. Being virtuous and acting virtuously implies having the right intentions, finding the right circumstances and goal, and also having the right emotions.

Student: Virtuous action has strict requirements.

Teacher: It does, and virtue is something hard to obtain, but not impossible.

Student: We have looked into the ideal of the perfectly virtuous person.

Teacher: Yes, and that has something to do with the principle of the unity of the virtues.

Student: I understand that this was already a concern for Socrates.

Teacher: The principle of the unity of the virtues represents an ideal. However, philosophers accept that many people can have some but not all virtues. The Stoics defend the ideal of the wise man.

Student: Aquinas states that virtue cannot be misused.

Teacher: That is correct. Virtue is something good in itself and it is also a goal, and therefore it cannot be misused, otherwise it would not be perfectly good.

Student: We have discussed the differences between moral and intellectual virtues, a distinction which is clearly established by Aristotle. I wonder if the moral virtues which he mentions exhaust the varieties of moral virtues?

Teacher: Some of the virtues he mentions are clearly central. Some of them had been mentioned by Plato, for instance, in the *Republic*. Justice, courage and temperance are clearly central moral virtues.

It is also clear that generosity in general is something essential for Aristotle and that it is connected to other virtues which he analyzes, like magnificence. Honor is also important for Aristotle, as well as certain social skills which are related to other virtues, like friendliness and being witty, in addition to mildness, which implies a control of anger.

Student: Controlling anger is a very important virtue in a social context, and it is central for our own self-perfection. Aristotle also mentions truthfulness, which is very significant in social dealings. It reminds us of Kant's ethical principles.

Teacher: In addition to the moral virtues, Aristotle develops the theory of the intellectual virtues. Prudence is most important, and also understanding and comprehension.

Student: Aquinas accepts most of what Aristotle has to say about the virtues, and he elaborates on the cardinal and theological virtues.

Teacher: That is correct. The theory of the cardinal virtues was developed in the Middle Ages, and Aquinas elaborates on it. He also develops the theory of the theological virtues, as virtues that are exclusively infused by God, rather than being acquired by our own merit. They concern the afterlife and the vision of God in the afterlife. He also considers some moral virtues as being infused by God.

Student: We have looked into the questions of habit and virtue as a mean.

Teacher: The question of the mean characterizes Aristotle's understanding of virtue. He holds that virtue is a mean between two extremes. For instance, courage is a mean between foolhardiness and cowardice. However, we cannot use a rigid mathematical formula to determine the mean, which has to be calculated according to the agent of the action, and in some cases, virtue is not the exact mean, but perhaps closer to one of the extremes. Virtue is a question of practical fine-tuning. Naturally, habit is central because it provides the experience which allows us to deal with concrete situations, and it ensures that virtuous behavior becomes easier and rooted in us. Virtue implies a coordination between our rational faculties and also our emotions, and stressing habit is an important part of that understanding of virtue. Philosophers who do not consider that the emotions have anything positive to contribute to our ethical behavior also tend not to stress the need for the habitual practice of virtuous acts.

Student: Friendship is a central concern for philosophers who wrote on ethics and also virtue.

Teacher: Friendship is a central concern for philosophers like Plato, Aristotle and Cicero, and also later philosophers. It is clear that it is something that closely binds human beings. To seek other human beings to share experiences and knowledge seems to be a feature of human nature. Aristotle and Cicero emphasize the fact that true friendship is based on virtue and not utility. Even today, we would not consider those who are merely useful to us as true friends, much as we would be grateful to them. Friendship implies companionship and the exercise of several virtues, such as courage, trust, benevolence, truthfulness and justice.

Student: I understand how friendship, and our tendency to seek friends, indicates certain features of human nature, namely its goodness and tendency towards sociability, while also providing essential opportunities to perfect human nature by way of virtuous behavior.

Teacher: Yes, and Cicero, who greatly values friendship, also thinks of virtue as something natural, like a second nature that follows reason. It is something that requires practice but it is rooted in human nature.

Student: The connection between theory and practice, reason and the emotions, is a central aspect to naturalistic virtue ethics.

At the same time, the Stoic approach to virtue can be very tempting, as being more straightforward. Is it possible to view virtue solely based on wisdom and knowledge, to the exclusion of the emotions, which can perturb us in our moral decisions?

Teacher: The emotions are part of human nature. Rather than setting them aside, it is better to harness them for moral goodness, a view that is defended by Aristotle and also Aquinas. For the British moralists and empiricists such as Hume, too, the emotions are an essential foundation for ethical behavior and moral character.

It would be more straightforward to associate virtue exclusively with knowledge, but including the emotions means taking account of the whole of human nature. This seems a more realistic and also a more productive approach to virtue ethics, even if the sole reliance on the principle of knowledge seems tempting.

Student: I understand the centrality of the emotions to virtue theory and virtue ethics, as part of a rounded conception of human nature.

Moreover, we can think of the accomplishments of human nature within various fields, for instance, epistemological, or aesthetic, but with reference to our common living, virtue ethics remains an essential approach to ethics.

Teacher: Virtue as a philosophical ethical theory remains as relevant today as it was in ancient Greece or medieval Europe. With regard to virtue ethics, we can establish connections with other disciplines, such as psychology, which would focus on character traits and the need to develop them. These traits are studied as part of a branch of psychology which is known as positive psychology, and they are also studied in moral psychology. Philosophy looks at virtue in more theoretical ways, but it offers a fundamental justification for ethical behavior and practical ways to implement it. It is not possible to do away with questions of character within ethics and therefore any ethical theory should take account of virtue ethics. Virtue ethics is also founded on human nature and reveals the perfection of human nature in its moral aspect.

Student: Is there a problem with the fact that virtue can change according to time and place, thus relativizing virtue ethics?

Teacher: It is true that certain observations regarding virtue made by Aristotle no longer apply. However, central features of his virtue ethics remain valid today, such as the general idea of the contribution of virtue to the common good, and individual self-perfection. The virtues mentioned by Aristotle and later by Aquinas, for instance, remain valid.

Even today, different cultures may focus on particular virtues. For instance, Eastern cultures may focus more on filial devotion, whereas we find a more individualistic approach to family life in the Western tradition, but the essential character of virtue as serving others while perfecting oneself remains among its essential features.

Student: The question of pleasure and happiness can also seem a little divisive in our approach to virtue ethics. Perhaps this also shows a tension between individual benefit and benefiting others.

Teacher: It would seem that if virtue involves pleasure, it benefits ourselves more than others. However, Aristotle does not see it that way. Instead, he holds that taking pleasure in acting virtuously means effortlessness and the interiorization of virtue, which is the culmination of a process of being educated towards virtuous behavior. Virtue and pleasure need not be at odds. The fact that virtue benefits ourselves as well as others should also not pose a problem.

Student: Contemporary philosophers have added to the number of virtues described and analyzed by Aristotle. We can think of tolerance as an important virtue—as well as patience and modesty, which were mentioned by Aquinas—for instance.

Teacher: There is still much to be studied and developed. Nevertheless, the foundations established by ancient, medieval and modern philosophers remain central to contemporary reflections on virtue ethics.